Alphaville

CINÉ-FILES: The French Film Guides
Series Editor: Ginette Vincendeau

From the pioneering days of the Lumière brothers' Cinématographe in 1895, France has been home to perhaps the most consistently vibrant film culture in the world, producing world-class directors and stars, and a stream of remarkable movies, from popular genre films to cult avant-garde works. Many of these have found a devoted audience outside France, and the arrival of DVD is now enabling a whole new generation to have access to contemporary titles as well as the great classics of the past.

The Ciné-Files French Film Guides build on this welcome new access, offering authoritative and entertaining guides to some of the most significant titles, from the silent era to the early 21st century. Written by experts in French cinema, the books combine extensive research with the author's distinctive, sometimes provocative perspective on each film. The series will thus build up an essential collection on great French classics, enabling students, teachers and lovers of French cinema both to learn more about their favourite films and make new discoveries in one of the world's richest bodies of cinematic work.

Ginette Vincendeau

The first Ciné-Files, publishing 2005, are:
Alphaville (Jean-Luc Godard, 1965) – Chris Darke
Les Diaboliques (Henri-Georges Clouzot, 1955) – Susan Hayward
La Haine (Mathieu Kassovitz, 1995) – Ginette Vincendeau
La Reine Margot (Patrice Chéreau, 1994) – Julianne Pidduck

Forthcoming Ciné-Files include:
Amélie (Jean-Pierre Jeunet, 2001) – Isabelle Vanderschelden
La Règle du jeu (Jean Renoir, 1939) – Keith Reader
Le Corbeau (Henri-Georges Clouzot, 1943) – Judith Mayne
Casque d'or (Jacques Becker, 1952) – Sarah Leahy
Cléo de 5 à 7 (Agnès Varda, 1961) – Valerie Orpen
Rififi (Jules Dassin, 1955) – Alastair Phillips
La Grande illusion (Jean Renoir, 1937) – Martin O'Shaughnessy
Un chien andalou (Luis Buñuel, 1929) – Elza Adamowicz
À bout de souffle (Jean-Luc Godard, 1960) – Ramona Fotiade

Alphaville

(Jean-Luc Godard, 1965)

Chris Darke

I.B. TAURIS
LONDON · NEW YORK

Published in 2005 by I.B.Tauris & Co. Ltd
6 Salem Road, London W2 4BU
175 Fifth Avenue, New York NY 10010
ibtauris.com

Copyright © Chris Darke, 2005

The right of Chris Darke to be identified as the author of this work has been asserted by him in accordance with the Copyright, Designs and Patents Act 1988.

All rights reserved. Except for brief quotations in a review, this book, or any part thereof, may not be reproduced, stored in or introduced into a retrieval system, or transmitted, in any form or by any means, electronic, mechanical, photocopying, recording or otherwise, without the prior written permission of the publisher.

ISBN: 1 84511 218 0 (hb)
EAN: 978 1 84511 218 9 (hb)
ISBN: 1 85043 986 9 (pb)
EAN: 978 1 85043 986 8 (pb)

A full CIP record for this book is available from the British Library

Typeset in Minion by Dexter Haven Associates Ltd, London
Printed and bound in Great Britain by TJ International Ltd, Padstow, Cornwall

Contents

'A strong imagination brings on the event' say the scholars. I am one of those who are very much affected by the imagination. Everyone feels its impact, but some are knocked over by it.

Michel de Montaigne

For LS

Acknowledgements

Thanks to:

Charles Bitsch, Raoul Coutard, John Mackenzie, Chris Marker, Chris Petit and Peter Whitehead for answering my questions.
Joe Lawlor and Christine Molloy (aka 'Desperate Optimists') for photographic evidence that *Alphaville* exists.
Robin ('Scanner') Rimbaud for invasive sound-surgery.
Belinda Guidi for the images of her tribute to *Alphaville* sculpted in light.
Michael Temple and Michael Witt for making material available.
Ginette Vincendeau for asking me to write this book, and her patience throughout.
Kieron Corless, Gareth Evans, Min Lee, Yann Perreau, Libby Saxton, Owen Saxton and Ben Slater for their advice, encouragement and support.
The staff at the Bibliothèque du film in Paris, the British Film Institute (BFI) Library and The British Library.

Synopsis

Having travelled through space in his Ford Galaxy, secret agent Lemmy Caution arrives from the Outerlands in Alphaville, the capital city of a distant planet. His mission is to find Professor von Braun (aka Leonard Nosferatu), a renegade scientist from the Outerlands who presides tyrannically over the city, which he controls through a supercomputer, Alpha 60. Disguised as Ivan Johnson, a reporter from the *Figaro-Pravda* newspaper, Lemmy checks in at his hotel, where he is met by the professor's daughter, Natasha von Braun, who is to be his guide. Natasha is an attractive 'Second Class Programmer' but Lemmy finds her odd; she doesn't know the meaning of the word 'love'.

Lemmy's first objective is to find Henry Dickson, a former Outerlands agent who had been sent on a similar mission to Lemmy's but never returned. In failing health, Dickson is living in the squalid Red Star hotel. On his deathbed, he explains to Lemmy that Alphaville is a highly advanced technocracy that no longer has any use for poets and artists. Giving Lemmy a book of poetry, Dickson instructs him to destroy Alpha 60, and then dies. Lemmy joins Natasha at a lecture given by Alpha 60, and together they go to a gala reception which the professor is attending and which includes the execution of dissidents as entertainment. Lemmy tries to talk to the professor but is beaten up by his bodyguards.

When Lemmy comes to, he is being dragged down corridors on his way to be interrogated by Alpha 60. The computer asks him a series of questions, and while it works out the answers Lemmy is free to go. He is shown around the computer's inner sanctum by the Chief Engineer, and during his guided tour, war is declared on the Outerlands. Returning to his hotel, Lemmy finds Natasha waiting for him. As they share breakfast he asks her if she recognises any of the words in the book of poems that Dickson gave him.

She is troubled by the memories that certain words stir in her, and Lemmy discovers that she was born not in Alphaville but in Neuva York. He tells her that he has fallen in love with her and that they must leave together for the Outerlands. They share a rhapsodic moment of love before the police arrive to haul Lemmy off for further interrogation.

Shooting his way out of the interrogation room, Lemmy goes looking for Professor von Braun. As he leaves he sees Natasha being dragged, struggling, into the building. Lemmy tells the professor to leave with him for the Outerlands but von Braun refuses, instead offering Lemmy the chance to stay and work with him in Alphaville. Lemmy kills him, firing bullets into the control panels of Alpha 60 for good measure. As the city starts to self-destruct Lemmy searches for Natasha, who he finds in the nerve centre of Alpha 60. The inhabitants of Alphaville stagger around them as the couple escape to Lemmy's car, which he pilots away from the city and towards the Outerlands. Lemmy tells Natasha not to look back and slowly, hesitantly, as if fighting to recover long-repressed words, she says – 'I love you.'

Introduction

Je suis Godard

Towards the end of *Alphaville*, the intergalactic tough guy Lemmy Caution finds himself face to face with the technocratic ruler of the city, Professor von Braun. 'Look at yourself,' the scientist comments laconically to the lizard-visaged secret agent; 'men of your type will soon be extinct. You'll become something worse than death. You'll become a legend.' It's hard not to hear in these words a prophecy of Godard's own fate as a filmmaker. To become a legend in one's own lifetime can be a kind of living death in which the artist, condemned to trade on past glories, is denied a future. Not that this has prevented Godard from continuing to work or from trading on the cachet of his legendary name. '"I am Godard" is a philosophical problem,' he observed in 1990; 'my current formula is "I am (*suis*) a dog and the dog follows (*suit*) Godard".'[1] And following the dog that follows the legend are still others, whose numbers, it must be said, have diminished over the years. But, then, it's been difficult to keep up with – let alone to follow – the career of an artist whose recent work has barely been distributed in the United Kingdom – or anywhere else, come to that – over the last 20 years.

To follow someone or something, whether a football team, a writer or a filmmaker, implies a degree of fidelity, the willingness to stick with them through the fallow periods as well as the triumphs. Which is just as well when it comes to Godard, especially from a British perspective. There are, no doubt, generations of Godard-followers: those who grew up with his films in the sixties and those who gave up or got lost along the way (and Godard did his utmost to lose his audience in the late 1960s), as well as those who stuck with him. But what of those who come late to Godard? Such latecomer-followers may have discovered his films in repertory cinemas or film classes, on television or through the invocation of his name by other directors. I write as someone whose interest in Godard was ignited in the mid-1980s, which, as luck would have it, was just around the time when his current work started to disappear from British screens. In the 16 years between the UK release of *Détective* in 1985 and *Éloge de l'amour/In Praise of Love* in 2001, Godard became a more or less historical figure, represented only by revivals of certain classics from his 1960s heyday: *À Bout de souffle/ Breathless* (1960, thrice re-released in 1988, 1996 and 2000), *Pierrot le fou* (1965, re-released in 1990), *Alphaville* (re-released in 1994), *Le Mépris/Contempt* (1963, re-released in 1996), *Bande à part/Band of Outsiders* (1964, re-released in 2001) and *Deux ou trois choses que je sais d'elle/Two or Three Things I Know About Her* (1967, re-released in 2001). Once acquired, the taste for Godard's early work is relatively easily satisfied but when one feels prepared to take on the harder fare of the later work – that's where the problems begin. That said, it's not even that easy to be a completist when it comes to the 1960s films; works such as *Le petit soldat/The Little Soldier* (1960), *Une Femme est une femme/A Woman is a Woman* (1961), *Les Carabiniers/The Riflemen* (1963), *Une Femme mariée/A Married Woman* (1964) and *Made in USA* (1966) have pretty much dropped out of circulation and hence don't really feature as part of the picture of that phase of his career. The stronger the sense is that the picture is only partial the greater the desire becomes to complete it, to hunt out the missing pieces. This takes time and no little devotion, and, before you know it, a certain kind of *cinéphilia* has been developed in the pursuit of a sense of the work's continuity.

However, from the early 1990s a number of books and major shows began to reassess Godard, not just from the perspective of his illustrious past but also of his elusive present. In 1991 the Museum of Modern Art (MoMA) in New York presented 'Jean-Luc Godard: Son + Image 1974–1991', an exhibition explicitly focusing on Godard's little-known video work. The handsome publication that accompanied the show included important essays on the director by major French critics Serge Daney, Raymond Bellour, Philippe Dubois and Jacques Aumont that had not previously been translated into English.[2] In the years between the MoMA show and the full career retrospective at London's National Film Theatre in 2001, Godard's work also began to circulate in multiple-media formats. The huge undertaking of the eight-part video essay *Histoire(s) du cinéma (1988–1998)* that had occupied the director intermittently from the late 1980s through the best part of the 1990s saw the light of day as a series of videos, books and compact discs of the complete soundtrack. The soundworld of Godard's filmmaking, always richly individual, became an increasingly significant aspect of his work, and his sympathetic relationship with the German music label ECM and its director Manfred Eicher saw the release, in 1997, of a two-disc boxed set of the complete soundtrack of his 1990 film *Nouvelle Vague*. Ten years after the MoMA show, in June and July 2001, the National Film Theatre staged a complete career retrospective entitled 'Jean-Luc Godard: Master of Modern Cinema'. This major event was significant for a variety of reasons, not least of which was the number of people of all ages – followers old and new – who turned out for the screenings. In addition, there was a touring programme of selected films from the retrospective that visited regional cinemas, as well as an international conference held at Tate Modern and, ending the 16-year absence on British screens of his current work, a cinema release of Godard's most recent film *Éloge de l'amour*, which, contrary to expectations, was met with critical warmth. Godard, it appeared, was back.

One might say that, alongside *À Bout de souffle* and *Le Mépris*, *Alphaville* has become 'a Godard film for those who don't like Godard'. Like the others, *Alphaville* exists somehow apart from its director's legend while also contributing to it, playing the part of honourable exception to the rule of Godard's work being seen as difficult and intellectual fare. But this glib summary considers only a fraction of a phase in his work, a handful of films from the first ten years of a career that has lasted for the best part of half a century. And, while *Alphaville* belongs to that period of frantic creativity that characterised Godard's work from his new wave period through to his abdication from commercial filmmaking after May 1968, it can now be viewed though the long lens of history. Which is to say that, while the film can be examined in the context of its time, it also requires the wider context provided by the so-called 'Godard renaissance' of the last decade. My approach in this book, then, is a fairly traditional kind of 'auteur criticism', but of a kind that's ever so slightly warped. One of the classic characteristics of such criticism is to place a director's films into an orderly corpus, hence to construct an idea of the body of work, the artist's oeuvre. No one can doubt that such a thing exists when it comes to Godard; it's just that so much of it has been kept from British viewers. In making connections across the Godard oeuvre and introducing other, less well-known works, I hope this book might provide, even if only partially, something akin to a 'Users' Guide to Godard' together with a more elaborate investigation of *Alphaville*.

Chapter 1 starts by setting *Alphaville* in the context of its production and introduces some of the cast and crew; in 'Dystopia discovered and described', 'Paris: city of the future' and 'From no-place to non-place', I explore the film's 'dystopian' vision of Paris. The section in Chapter 2 entitled 'The robots are already here!', further examines *Alphaville*'s dystopia as it relates to ideas about modernisation and technology that were current in 1960s France. Most of my references in these sections are drawn from fiction and non-fiction of the early to mid-20th century – that is, roughly contemporary with *Alphaville*. The greater part of the second chapter examines the many ways in which *Alphaville* can be seen to be 'a film about light', as Godard has described it. *Alphaville* now takes its place as a film in which elements of Godard's approach to cinema cohere with a clarity that only hindsight reveals, and such hindsight comes through works made since the 1960s. It makes sense in writing about *Alphaville* not to strand the film in the context of its time but to point up affinities with less well-known later works such as *Histoire(s) du cinéma*, *Allemagne année 90 neuf zéro/Germany Year 90 Nine Zero* (1991) and *Éloge de l'amour* (2001), and this is the task of the final chapter, '*Alphaville*: the afterlife', in which I also describe some of the many tributes and reassessments that the film has generated in its wake.

The trouble with writing about Godard is that the director has all the best lines. With this in mind, I haven't stinted on dipping into his abundant supply of aphorisms and *aperçus*, which I call upon to provoke my argument and ideas. While writing this book I was asked more than once which film I was working on, and when I replied '*Alphaville*' the response, more often than not, was 'it's one of my favourite movies' or 'I love that film'. I hope that those who rate the film highly will find enough in these pages in the way of surprises, and perhaps even insights, to add to their enjoyment. For others less familiar with Godard, welcome to *Alphaville*.

Notes

1 'La Télévision fabrique de l'oubli', *Actuel* 136, 1990, in A. Bergala (ed.), *Jean-Luc Godard par Jean-Luc Godard*, vol. 2, *1984–1998* (Cahiers du cinéma, Paris,

1998), p. 241. (All translations from the French are mine unless an English-language source is indicated; CD.)

2 Bandy, Mary Lea and Bellour, Raymond (eds), *Jean-Luc Godard: Son + Image, 1974–1991* (Museum of Modern Art, New York, 1992). Other significant publications contributing to the 'Godard renaissance' since the 1990s include: Williams, James S., Witt, Michael and Temple, Michael (eds), *Forever Godard* (Black Dog Publishing, London, 2004); Temple, Michael and Williams, James S. (eds), *The Cinema Alone: Essays on the Work of Jean-Luc Godard 1985–2000* (Amsterdam University Press, Amsterdam, 2000); Sterrit, David, *The Films of Jean-Luc Godard: Seeing the Invisible* (Cambridge University Press, Cambridge, 1999); Farocki, Harun and Silverman, Kaja, *Speaking About Godard* (New York University Press, New York, 1998) and Dixon, Wheeler Winston, *The Films of Jean-Luc Godard* (State University of New York Press, New York, 1997).

1 Godardville

Alphaville exists

Alphaville, São Paulo, 2003 (photograph courtesy of Desperate Optimists)

Seven and a half miles from the heart of São Paulo there is a gated community that houses 30,000 of the city's richest and most security-conscious residents, many of whom travel by helicopter to work among the 17 million other inhabitants of the world's third largest city. According to *The Washington Post*, 'At night, on "TV Alphaville", residents can view their maids going home for the evening, when all exiting employees are patted down and searched in front of a live video feed.'[1] In his account of 'a walled city where the privileged live behind electrified fences patrolled by a private army of 1,100', the *Post*'s correspondent failed to discover which keen ironist had named the development after the film by Jean-Luc Godard.[2] Nor, I suppose, would it have been much appreciated had the reporter, as he flew low over the teeming *favelas*, the prisons and choked highways, casually asked his host, a CEO and Alphaville resident, 'You do realise you're living in a movie, don't you?'

Developed by the Alphaville Urbanismo Corporation in the 1970s, Alphaville São Paulo 'resembles its fictional namesake in elaborate and all-encompassing surveillance techniques', writes an American professor of urban studies, 'including high walls, hidden cameras and alarm systems … The Alphaville gym specialises in self-defence and is called CIA.'[3] The facts about the development get better, or still worse, depending on whether one prefers dystopia to remain firmly in the realms of fiction or to come, fully-fledged, to life:

> To advertise Alphaville, the company sponsored some episodes of a popular prime-time Brazilian soap opera whose leading male character is an architect. The architect and his mistress visit Alphaville where, according to Brazil's *Gazeta Mercantil*, the characters exalt the safety, freedom and planning of the place, comparing it to the neighbourhoods shown in US films.[4]

And so … Godard's film about a city of the future, shot on location in the Paris of the mid-1960s, has endowed not just one but 30 'gated communities' in Brazil with its name.[5] And reality, having provided fiction with the raw material for its most dystopian scenarios, returns the compliment by materialising them. The back and forth between image and reality is dizzying: from CCTV to soap opera, from European art cinema to aspirational Hollywood, and back again. Where does the utopian projection end and dystopian reality begin? We might call it, with a certain queasiness, the 'Alphaville effect'. But surely this is only an accident of naming, a sick joke? Are the 'Alphas' paying to inhabit their top-security luxury lock-up only so-called compared to the *favela*-dwelling 'Omegas'? How long before Alphaville becomes a suburb of Los Angeles, a satellite of Mumbai? As the oracular tones of the supercomputer Alpha 60 remind us at the beginning of Godard's film, there are indeed times when 'reality becomes too complex for oral transmission. But legend gives it a form by which it pervades the whole world.' In the face of a reality too complex, too ironically dystopian, too straightforwardly ugly to address directly, let us attend to the legend.

Tarzan *versus* IBM

Legend has it that *Alphaville* almost didn't exist. Interviewed in September 1964, Godard alluded to a forthcoming project: 'I've a film to make in December with [Eddie] Constantine. I've no idea at all what I'm going to do.'[6] The film producer André Michelin (a scion of the famous French tyre manufacturing family) had proposed to the director a film featuring Eddie Constantine, who had been a star of French cinema during the 1950s playing the FBI tough guy Lemmy Caution, and both director and star had agreed. However, one of the director's options at the time was to drop, or at least delay, the project in favour of making a film in the United States. The project in question was *Bonnie and Clyde*, which François Truffaut had been interested in making but had to abandon when the financing came together for his own excursion into science fiction, an adaptation of Ray Bradbury's 1953 novel *Fahrenheit 451*. In a letter to the scriptwriters, Robert Benton and David Newman, Truffaut mentioned that he had 'taken the liberty of passing [the script] on to Jean-Luc Godard'.[7] Godard met with the producers in November that year. 'What it boiled down to was this,' Benton and Newman recalled: 'he had been supposed to start another film in Paris next month but he didn't feel much like doing it. He liked the script of *Bonnie and Clyde* very much and thought he would do that. In three weeks from now.'[8] The film Godard 'didn't feel much like doing' was obviously the as yet untitled Eddie Constantine project, but let us stay with Benton and Newman's recollection of that meeting for a moment, if only to entertain the wonderfully improbable idea of Godard in Hollywood.

> Our producers went white. But, they said, we were not ready, that is, there was no deal, no financing, no studio. Godard said it didn't matter; we immediately agreed with him. Why not? He said, that day, two things which are forever writ upon our memories: 'If it happens in life, it can happen in a movie.' This to the producer's objection that the key elements might not be perfectly pulled together in three week's time. And, 'We can make this film anywhere; we can make it in Tokyo.' This in response to the producer's objection that

weather conditions were not right in Texas for shooting at this time of year. A call to the weather bureau in Dallas was made. Strong possibilities of precipitation were predicted. 'You see?' said the producer. 'I am speaking cinema and you are speaking meteorology,' said Godard.[9]

Bonnie and Clyde as directed by Godard was not to be. Back in France, where his reputation was based at least in part on being the most extreme of the new wave innovators, Godard's singular approach to filmmaking could also cause problems, and *Alphaville* was a case in point. Raoul Coutard, the director of photography on all but one of Godard's 1960s films, remembers how, in order to get a film off the ground, the state film body, the Centre National de la Cinématographie (CNC), required not only a screenplay but a detailed shot breakdown known as a *découpage*:

It had to specify things like 'wide shot', 'medium shot', 'close up'. Everything was very precise. So a production plan was made and signed by the filmmaker, the director of production and the cinematographer in order to show that the film could be made in the time allotted. But Jean-Luc didn't work from a screenplay so he got his assistant to write one and the *découpage* was made from that. But it was a fake document.[10]

The problems arose because *Alphaville* was conceived as a Franco-German co-production. Godard's assistant director on the film, Charles Bitsch, takes up the story:

Eddie Constantine was very popular in Germany and his films made money there, so German producers were always on the lookout to co-produce a film with the French starring Eddie Constantine. When I started to work on the preparation for the film there was no screenplay, which was often the case with Godard. I tried, without success, to get him to write three or four pages for me so that I could get to work. Michelin was also impatient for a screenplay which he needed to set up the co-production with his German partners. Finally, Godard asked me to write the screenplay. I asked him to put me on the right tracks and all I got by way of a response was that he lent me three novels by Peter Cheyney, who created the character of Lemmy Caution. He told me that I only had to read them and write a story in the same genre. So I wrote thirty pages, which Godard gave to Michelin as the screenplay. I kept quiet about who'd written the screenplay as it had landed in the hands of the Germans who signed a contract with Michelin on the strength of it and the film went into production. Of course, Godard didn't use a single word of what I'd written and he was right not to. On the other hand, there were serious consequences for Michelin. When the Germans saw some of the rushes and discovered the scam they pulled out of the co-production and demanded to be reimbursed for the first payment made when the contract was signed.[11]

Nevertheless, by January 1965 Godard had begun shooting a project initially known as *Tarzan versus IBM*, which the director had described in a questionnaire published in *Cahiers du cinéma* the same month as 'an experimental art-house adventure film'.[12] The film was shot between January and February, and the finished work, now entitled *Alphaville, une étrange aventure de Lemmy Caution*, won the prize for Best Film at the Berlin Film Festival and was released in Paris on 5 May, where it played until August and attracted some 160,000 spectators. It's worth considering the facts and figures behind this brief exposition. Five months from filming to release represents a speed of production that is unimaginable in filmmaking today and was exceptional then. Working quickly and cheaply, Godard turned out films at an astonishing rate throughout the 1960s. *Alphaville* was his ninth in the five years since his debut with *À Bout de souffle* in 1960, and in the same year as *Alphaville* he also made two others, *Pierrot le fou* and *Masculin-Féminin*. By 1968, the year in which he abandoned commercial cinema for a more politically radical form of filmmaking, Godard had made a total of 18 features and eight shorts.

Alphaville has the reputation of being something of an anomaly among Godard's pre-1968 films. His sole feature-length foray into science fiction and one of his few encounters with a star with major box-office appeal, in this case Eddie Constantine (three years earlier Godard had worked with Brigitte Bardot in *Le Mépris*, which proved to be a box-office success in terms of Godard's public, less so in terms of Bardot's), it's a film that has been strangely neglected by critics. According to Marc Cerisuelo, the author of a handy French monograph on the director, *Alphaville* is the most 'explicitly "secondary" of his works' and is described as such because of the presence of Eddie Constantine as Lemmy Caution, a stalwart of French thrillers of the 1950s derived from the novels by Peter Cheyney.[13] Punching and shooting his way through *Alphaville*'s sepulchral labyrinth of corridors and staircases, Lemmy Caution is truly an alien in Godardville (a quotation of himself as well as an intruder in 'The Capital of Pain'), and Constantine's popular persona is, as Cerisuelo puts it, 'pulverised' by the Godardian aesthetic.[14] But, even given the unusual generic hybrid of film noir and science fiction (which nevertheless proved highly influential), it was hardly as if Godard hadn't essayed other such unlikely combinations before. In fact, such hybrid forms were a mainstay, if not a formula, in Godard's sixties phase. And one can talk about formula here in the strict generic sense. How else to explain the 'Tarzan versus IBM' cartoon-strip equation behind *Alphaville* other than as a knowing nod in the direction of Japanese monster movies of the *King Kong versus Godzilla* variety? But it was also as a straightforward description of the film's colliding elements: Tarzan – that's to say, Lemmy Caution – going head to head with Alpha 60, aka IBM. Godard used such suggestive shorthand repeatedly, describing *Une Femme est une femme* as 'a neo-realist musical' and Michel Piccoli's character in *Le Mépris* (1963), the vacillating screenwriter Paul Javal, as 'a character from Howard Hawks in a film by Resnais'.[15] It requires no great stretch of the imagination to credit (or blame) Godard for having invented the so-called 'high-concept pitch', in which an idea for a film is given as a sure-fire generic recipe: *Alien*, for example, equals '*Jaws* in outer space'.

The sheer pace and variety of Godard's output has repercussions for anyone examining a single film from this period. You can't really deal with one without broaching some of the others. The question is: which others? An answer lies in examining what Godard was using his cinema for in the 1960s. There is a popular conception of the director as an inveterate collagist, adept at reassembling moments from film history that he had amassed, first as a young *cinéphile* at Henri Langlois' Cinémathèque Française, then as a critic on *Cahiers du cinéma*, subsequently restaging them with a new cast on the streets of Paris. This caricature has a grain of truth to it, but his form of *ciné-bricolage* rapidly became refined into a unique cinematic method. Godard's principal subject has always been cinema itself. In this respect, his is a deeply self-conscious, reflexive approach to filmmaking; every element of his films' fabric is layered like a palimpsest. The choice of black and white film in *Alphaville* has a host of connotations, as does the casting and the use of certain genres. These choices are steeped in an understanding of film history, which, when brought to bear on the object of Godard's interest, inflects his cinema's gaze with a unique kind of double vision, one famously condensed in his own self-assessment: 'I need to show and show me showing.'[16] In order to isolate *Alphaville* within Godard's output in the 1960s one must nevertheless elect certain films as companion pieces. One way of doing so is to propose the following: that, during the 1960s, Godard was, first and foremost, a Parisian filmmaker. It's hardly a controversial claim; after all, of the 18 features made between 1960 and 1968, only four –

Le petit soldat, Les Carabiniers, Le Mépris and *Pierrot le fou* – were shot outside the city. For *Alphaville*, Godard built no sets and commissioned no special effects. Having neither the budget nor the inclination to do so, he simply took to the streets of Paris in 1965 using what was to hand, choosing to focus on the tell-tale details of the architectural and technological fabric of the city in order to anatomise a future already latent in the present. But this attempt to illuminate the presence of the future required that this sci-fi city be filmed in the light of the past, the haunted *chiaroscuro* of German expressionism and the monochrome of film noir.

Godardville – that's to say, Paris in the late 1950s and 1960s, during the period of its modernisation – is full to bursting with signs. Apartments are packed with objects, newspapers and magazines. Streets are full of people, cars, fashion and advertising. And then, of course, there is cinema, spilling off the screen onto the streets and lapping back again in the same movement. One can approach Godard's sixties films as a kind of scattershot sociological portrait of the period and tick off the brand names, list the cultural figureheads who crop up (director Jean-Pierre Melville in *À Bout de souffle*, philosopher Brice Parrain in *Vivre sa vie*, writer Roger Leenhardt in *Une Femme mariée*), as well as sketch the political *parti pris* and thereby arrive at a catalogue of details that are part and parcel of the speed and pace with which Godard made his films, as if their object, nothing less than modern life itself, might otherwise escape too quickly from apprehension by the cinema. So there is a sense in which these films now require footnotes and lend themselves readily to such dutiful annotation, to the extent that their subject – cinema – risks being obscured. I point out this problem only to emphasise that, while it is indeed possible to get lost in the density of sociological detail in Godard's films of the 1960s, one should not lose sight of the fact that, along with the documentary aspect, there is always spectacle, the use of fiction and genre. And this is why, in quite another respect, *Alphaville* is something of an anomaly in this period of work. The details of everyday life that are displayed, documented and dramatised in other films (two in particular stand out, *Une Femme mariée* and *Deux ou trois choses que je sais d'elle*, to which I shall return later) are, in *Alphaville*, either absent – no brand names, no media, no advertising – or are abstracted to such an extent that they no longer appear to belong to the period in which they were filmed. The success of Godard's 'abstraction' may go some way to explain why *Alphaville* has managed to find a life beyond the specificities of its period that has been denied to the other films, managing to float free of its real location into the rarified realm of the 'cinematic city', that other environment unique to the 20th century that, X-rayed from the stone and steel of a real city, returns to stick to its skin.

Who's who in the Capital of Pain

The crew that Godard gathered for *Alphaville* included some of his most trusted collaborators, among them the cinematographer Raoul Coutard, editor Agnès Guillemot and the make-up artist Jackie Reynal ('Godard didn't like make-up').[17] Each saw long service with the director throughout the 1960s, Reynal taking care of Karina's face-paint ('Anna adored make-up') from *Une Femme est une femme* (1961) up to *La Chinoise* (1967), and

Exiled in Alphaville: Henry Dickson (Akim Tamiroff, top left); mad doctor, Nazi scientist, Professor von Braun (Howard Vernon, top right); errant daughter, soul sister, Natasha von Braun (Anna Karina, bottom left); Orpheus in a trenchcoat, Lemmy Caution (Eddie Constantine, bottom right).

Guillemot cutting all but two of his feature films between *Le petit soldat* (1960) and *Weekend* (1967).[18]

Raoul Coutard (director of photography)

Coutard's contribution as cinematographer was crucial to Godard's films of the 1960s and he was the most long-standing of the director's technical collaborators, shooting all but one of the features from *À Bout de souffle* (1960) to *Weekend* (1967), the exception being *Masculin-Féminin* (1966); he would also work intermittently on later films, including *Passion* (1982) and *Prénom Carmen/First Name: Carmen* (1983). Coutard was a former soldier and photographer who was willing and able to shoot quickly, in documentary style, often filming in available light with a hand-held camera. The striking reportage look that Coutard bought to the cinematography of *À Bout de souffle* led to a long and fruitful collaboration with Godard, which encompassed many different styles of colour and black and white cinematography and was always experimental in its pursuit of new ways of shooting and developing film. As Coutard recounts:

> One of Jean-Luc's ways of doing things was to try with each film to do something he hadn't done before. He'd say, 'I don't make films, I make cinema.' What he meant was he wasn't telling a story. Another approach of his at that time was to say: 'When we shoot in black and white we use the Academy format (1:1.33) and when we shoot in colour we use Cinemascope.' This was his guiding principle and each time he worked there was practically always the temptation to do something that was technically new. So, with *Alphaville*, because a lot of it takes place at night, we decided to use the system of shooting we'd used for the night scenes in *À Bout de souffle*, that's to say, to use the English HPS film stock and to develop it in a photographic bath which, at the time, was used by photographers to double the sensitivity of the stock without the grain becoming too enlarged.[19]

For Godard, *Alphaville* was in part an experiment in seeing how far he could push black and white film when shooting in available, artificial light with little or no extra lighting. Coutard considers the process and pitfalls of such an experiment further in the next chapter.

The cast for *Alphaville* included Eddie Constantine, who had been a major star throughout the 1950s, and Godard's *actrice-fétiche* Anna Karina, for whom this was the fifth of six films in which she would star under his direction. In the years since *Alphaville*, Constantine has become something of a cinematic revenant. Like the supporting actors in the film, Howard Vernon and Akim Tamiroff, he is a reminder of another era of cinema, permanently entombed in his generic uniform of overcoat and trilby, forever recapitulating his tough-guy routines to the point when, late in his life, he needed only stand still and emit his trademark basilisk stare. There's a kind of pathos at work in this casting, most clearly exploited in the scene between Tamiroff and Constantine, which has only increased as the years have passed. Constantine may well have been a major star in the 1950s but, by the time he came to work with Godard, his star power was waning and he was prepared to reinvent, if not to overhaul completely, his screen persona which was derived largely from the character of Lemmy Caution. Vernon and Tamiroff come from a generation of second-role performers who, while never being stars in their own right, were what would now be called 'character actors', adept at donning a variety of different disguises in a range of films, from Hollywood spectaculars to big-budget international co-productions, from European art films to Z-grade genre pulp.

The Cast

Akim Tamiroff (Henry Dickson)

Legend has it that, in the 1930s, the make-up department of Paramount Studios kept a drawer marked 'Akim Tamiroff's Eyelids'. At that point in his varied career as an itinerant second-role character actor, Tamiroff (1899–1972) was known for the grotesque make-up he donned for films such as *The General Died at Dawn* (Lewis Milestone, 1936), but even such extravagant prostheses could not conceal the features that make any scene with him in worth watching and that had helped secure his career as an actor. In 1918 he was one of four applicants out of 500 to be admitted to the prestigious Moscow Art Theatre School, where Constantin Stanislawski was a teacher. The principal of the school, working his way through the hopeful ranks, spotted something in the young man's doleful aspect. 'You have interesting eyes,' he is reported to have told the 19-year-old native of Baku; 'you look as if you are suffering.'[20] Between 1932, when he started to work in American films (having jumped ship and stayed in the United States after a theatre tour), and his death 40 years later Tamiroff appeared in over 50 films, working six times with fellow Russian exile Milestone as well as with such other luminaries of classical Hollywood as Ruben Mamoulian, Ernst Lubitsch, Billy Wilder and Cecil B. De Mille. By the 1950s Tamiroff was working all over the world on films by Vittorio De Sica, Claude Chabrol and Jules Dassin. It was with Orson Welles that he found something akin to a place in a stock company, appearing in *Confidential Report/Mr Arkadin* (1955), *Touch of Evil* (1958) and *The Trial* (1963), as well as playing Sancho Panza in the director's film adaptation of *Don Quixote,* which he had been filming, on and off, since 1957.[21] It's from Welles' expressionistic vision of Kafka that Tamiroff appears to have wandered in when we first meet him in *Alphaville.* When he pokes his head, somnolently suspicious, in the window of the shabby reception of the Red Star hotel it's as though he'd taken a wrong turning somewhere in the totalitarian labyrinth of *The Trial,* only to find that he'd arrived in another dystopian maze, a further suburb of hell. What does Tamiroff do in his scene in *Alphaville*? He gazes blankly at his fellow secret agent, smokes a cigarette, collapses on a staircase, delivers some bronchial plot exposition, fumbles rhapsodically with a *séductrice* and expires while croaking to Lemmy: 'Destroy Alpha 60 … save those who weep' (see Appendix 1, Sequence 3). He steals the scene completely, reducing Constantine to second-role status just by looking at him. When Lemmy questions him on the staircase of the Red Star hotel, Godard lifts details from the moment in *The Trial* when K (Anthony Perkins) happens upon three policemen in an interrogation room lit by a single, bare bulb that, set swinging back and forth, throws wildly elongated shadows. Godard's use of real locations echoes Welles' use of similar settings to conjure up a bleak environment of totalitarian brutalism, and the way that the police seem to materialise from nowhere in K's apartment at the beginning of the film is strongly reminiscent of the policeman's arrival in Lemmy's hotel room. Tamiroff's presence can be seen, therefore, as having provided Godard with an alibi to invoke Welles' vision of Kafka.

Howard Vernon (Professor von Braun)

As Professor von Braun, the Swiss actor Howard Vernon (1914–1996) got to play Godard's version of a Bond villain. The 007 connection is not as far-fetched as it might appear. Lemmy, after all, is secret agent 003, and von Braun is a ruthless technocrat with plans for interplanetary destruction who, in time-honoured fashion, attempts at the last minute to persuade Lemmy to join him in his diabolical plans. Vernon had also acted in Fritz Lang's last film *The Thousand Eyes of Dr Mabuse/Die Tausend Augen des Dr Mabuse* (1960), in which he played a maniacal henchman of Mabuse, the mysterious criminal mastermind who is being hunted by none other than Gert Fröbe (playing Chief Inspector Kras), the actor who was soon to find international fame as one of Bond's most memorable adversaries, the titular evil genius of *Goldfinger* (Guy Hamilton, 1964). Vernon was also associated with other roles, particularly those of Nazi officers and mad doctors. For French audiences Vernon was recognisable for his role as Werner von Ebrennac, the cultured, sensitive 'good German' in Jean-Pierre Melville's screen adaptation of the classic novel of French resistance, *Le Silence de la mer* (1949). This role led Vernon to don the uniform of the Wehrmacht officer numerous times, and his stiff, formal bearing and beady stare were well suited to such parts. Vernon also had a long, if hardly illustrious, career in horror cinema, specialising in playing unhinged physicians, and he became a favourite actor of the Spanish director Jesus Franco, the generalissimo of hack horror films such as *The Awful Dr Orlof /Gritos en la noche* (1962), for whom Vernon acted right up to his death. In an obituary, *Cahiers* recognised that the actor's presence had 'inescapably dignified serial-films, from B to Z grade, by injecting a suggestion of the cerebral while auteur films had, thanks to him, the slightly disreputable odour of Z grade pulp'.[22] In *Alphaville*, Vernon represents a piece of all-purpose casting the associations of which extend in several different directions at once – to Lang and Dr Mabuse, to Melville and the many screen Nazis the actor portrayed, but also to Lemmy Caution's own screen past, for Vernon had been Lemmy's first adversary in Constantine's screen debut, *La Môme vert-de-gris/Poison Ivy* (Bernard Borderie, 1952), playing the louche gangster Rudy Saltierra.

Anna Karina (Natasha von Braun)

Like Coutard, Karina is an inescapable part of Godard's early films. The couple had married in 1961, and between 1960 and 1967 they made seven feature films together – *Le petit soldat, Une Femme est une femme, Vivre sa vie, Bande à part, Alphaville, Pierrot le fou, Made in USA* – and one short – *Anticipation, ou l'amour en l'an 2000* – for the portmanteau film *Le plus vieux métier du monde/The World's Oldest Profession* (1966). Karina recalled the shooting of *Alphaville* in a recent interview:

> We never had a script. What was amazing at that time was that he went to London to a laboratory because there was this new kind of film and he went to learn about this. What he liked about it was that he didn't need to use a lot of light. [...] We had to make a lot of shots ... he was afraid of problems onscreen.[23]

When *Bande à part* was re-released in 2001 the press was more than happy to wax lyrical in recalling the enduring appeal of her films with Godard. Writing in *The Independent*, Kevin Jackson claimed her as representative of cinema's 'eternal feminine': 'Godard, saturated in the history of film, certainly insinuated that she was an avatar of that same feminine cinematic principle that had previously been made flesh in Louise Brooks and Marie Falconetti.'[24] Michael Atkinson, in *The Village Voice*, hymned

> the sad-eyed, raven-haired Guinevere of the international art film's *belle époque* [who] will always possess a hallowed place in movie history ...[Karina] defined Movieness by being all things to all witnesses: star, beauty, impulsive every-waif, director's *inamorata*, self-conscious movie image, genre spoofer, liberated gender-combat totem.[25]

There's a further aspect to Karina's enduring appeal that goes beyond the Parisian 'cool' associated with the new wave and its shorthand signifiers of cafés, cigarettes and pseudo-intellectual *badinage*: her 'everydayness'. And, of all the films she made with Godard, *Alphaville* is the one in which she is cast as a character who is outside the everyday and emphatically otherworldly. One might say that part of the film's appeal lies in watching Natasha become Anna, the brainwashed 'Second Class Programmer' slowly letting slip the *gamine* enchantress she is in Godard's other films.

Codename Orpheus: the strange adventures of Eddie Constantine

Eddie Constantine (1917–1993) had the sort of face that looked destined to be wedged between a snap-brim hat and the upturned collar of an overcoat. The American critic Manny Farber described it with cartoon vividness as resembling that of 'a bullfrog corrugated by a defective waffle iron'.[26] But it wasn't initially destined for the cinema. Born in 1917 to émigré Russian parents in Los Angeles, Edward Constantinewski trained to be an opera singer at the Vienna Conservatory. Throughout the 1930s and 1940s he performed internationally with swing bands and as a solo singer, and in the early 1950s he became the protégé of the legendary Parisian *chanteuse* Edith Piaf. (One can only wonder whether Constantine's singing career informed Godard's vision of him as a pulp incarnation of Orpheus, the singer of classical myth.) His highly popular persona as the French-speaking FBI agent Lemmy Caution was established in the mid-1950s with the commercial success of the films adapted from Peter Cheyney's novels. Of the 40 plus films Constantine made in France, his eight screen outings as Lemmy Caution began in 1952 with *La Môme vert-de-gris* and ended in 1965 with *Alphaville*, the subtitle of which, it's worth recalling, is 'a strange adventure of Lemmy Caution' – and for a large part of Constantine's popular audience the vision of Lemmy at large in Godardville must have been strange indeed. By 1965 Constantine's fortunes had dwindled somewhat since his heyday in the mid-1950s, but he retained a certain box-office appeal and, according to the actor, Godard 'wanted to make this film; he needed it. He thought that if he didn't shoot it he was never going to do anything again.'[27] Constantine also mentioned that the director's initial idea had been to make a vampire film, something alluded to in the film's subtitle with its nod towards Carl Theodor Dreyer's *Vampyr: l'étrange aventure de David Gray* (1932), as well as in the name Professor Leonard Nosferatu.[28]

Some of the groundwork for what was to become *Alphaville* had already been done. Godard appeared in a cameo role alongside Constantine and Anna Karina in Agnès Varda's *Cléo de 5 à 7/Cléo from 5 to 7* (1961), and went on to cast the actor as the personification of 'Sloth' – a film star so lazy he can't be bothered to undress a willing young starlet – in a 20-minute episode for the 'portmanteau' film *Les sept péchés capitaux/The Seven Deadly Sins* (1961), admitting that he would like the opportunity to work with the actor again. Another sketch, made for the film *RoGoPaG* (1962) and entitled *Le nouveau monde/The New World*, rehearsed some of the themes that would be developed in *Alphaville*. After an atomic explosion above Paris a man wakes up to discover that all those around him, including his girlfriend, have been subtly but irrevocably transformed, the world has changed and he is the last human left among a race of mutants.[29] In *Alphaville*, Constantine's persona was less 'pulverised' than purified, reduced to its essence. Godard referred to Constantine more than once as being like a 'block', and all the extraneous pediments that attached to Lemmy Caution – the whisky, dolly-birds and punch-ups – are either stripped away or thoroughly remodelled by the director.[30] Constantine explained that the traditional Lemmy Caution formula required 'five punch-ups and three girls' per film.[31] In *Alphaville*, Godard gives Lemmy a damsel in distress to pursue chastely and a trio of *séductrices* to brush away. Fight sequences are dispensed in 'homeopathic doses' or simply 'skipped over'[32] (Wim Wenders has described Constantine's fight scenes as being 'like dance sequences in a bad musical': choreography without conviction).[33] Raoul Coutard revealed, somewhat surprisingly, that Constantine was 'extremely maladroit, he was completely incapable of reloading a pistol'.[34] In scenes involving fist fights, Godard frequently leaves the violence to the viewer's imagination. When Lemmy is roughed up in a lift by von Braun's thugs, for example (see Appendix 1, Sequence 4), the scene becomes a literal 'knockabout', with Constantine being buffeted from one side of the frame to the other by unseen blows; or he abstracts its effect, filming Lemmy's fight in the hotel bathroom through its reflection in the mirror, or having him grapple with a blond heavy in an underground car park in a series of still images (then upping the ante by showing Lemmy's car buck and heave as he nonchalantly manoeuvres it over his assailant's head). While happy to be working with Godard, Constantine admitted that the director's unorthodox methods took a bit of getting used to:

> He was shooting, but without a story. So, for three days, I was walking the streets of Paris alone in my hat and raincoat and he was doing panoramic shots of the ultra-modern buildings of La Défense. But he still didn't have a story. Suddenly, after three days, he called me: 'I've got the story now, I'll write it.' He wrote in the morning from 9 to mid-day, at 2 we'd rehearse and then at 5 we'd shoot. We filmed one shot a day, but a shot of 5 to 6 minutes.[35]

Constantine also revealed what sounds like Godard's attempt to terrorise his cast into submission:

> He was very good to me, except for one time. I had a scene in which I had to slap a girl in a hotel. I slapped her as I'd learned to, so as not to hurt her and he said 'No, not like that. You're not John Wayne.' So I slapped her like he wanted and the girl was so stunned she could barely move. There was the mark of my hand on her cheek and she couldn't go on. But Godard still wasn't happy, so he showed me how to do it. He slapped me. You wouldn't believe it, he hurt me like no-one's ever hurt me and then he asked me if I was in pain and I said 'No, no, not at all.' I couldn't hear anything out of my left ear, I was completely paralysed, too.[36]

If Constantine's Caution persona is 'purified', the element of self-parody that was always implicit in it is heightened in *Alphaville*. For some, this was a parody too far. Arlette Elkaïm, in *Les Temps Modernes*, commented sardonically that 'to have heard [Lemmy Caution] pronounce, in penetrating tones, "I believe in the immediate promptings of my consciousness" and "the silence of these infinite spaces appalled me" will remain among the happiest memories of my life'.[37] In his other films, Constantine had played Lemmy with a nod and a somewhat ingratiating wink to the audience; Godard stripped away this element too. Lemmy *chez* Godard is a more sombre creature than was usually the case, and the comedy derives largely from the incongruous spectacle of Lemmy, at large and at a loss, in the city of Alphaville.

Godard was familiar with Constantine's persona from his days as a film critic. He had observed with delight how, in Jean Rouch's film *Moi, un noir* (1958), Lemmy Caution was revealed as a character available to be lifted and interpreted by others. Godard wrote twice on the film, describing it in *Cahiers* as 'the film to save French cinema'.[38] Rouch was an ethnographer by profession (it's interesting to recall that Godard was, nominally, a student of ethnography at the Sorbonne before cinema became his vocation) and had started making films as part of his research in the field. *Moi, un noir* was shot in the Nigerian town of Treichville, in which a group of young Africans Rouch had worked with and befriended improvised their own scenes. They did so by taking the names of film stars and characters: Edward G. Robinson, Dorothy Lamour, Tarzan, Eddie Constantine and Lemmy Caution. In a long essay on the film in *Cahiers*, Godard claimed that 'Rouch's originality lies in having made characters out of his actors', stating that 'all great fictions films tend towards documentary, just as all great documentaries tend towards fiction'.[39] In *À Bout de souffle*, shot in the same year that *Moi, un noir* was released, Godard made his 'documentary' on an actor – Jean-Paul Belmondo – playing a character – Humphrey Bogart – with the fiction emerging in the gap between the two. Constantine admitted that *Alphaville* was conceived to 'kill off' the Lemmy Caution character:

> It was Lemmy projected into a future world with which he was unable to cope. And we succeeded all too well. I never worked again in French films ... *Alphaville* destroyed the myth of Lemmy Caution for the French. The people who believed in me were suddenly told not to believe. I didn't know it then, but it was an end of career.[40]

The encounter between Lemmy Caution, the character from popular French film, and Godard, the auteur director with a *cinéphile* audience, had the predictable effect of alienating part of Constantine's popular audience. Godard was clearly aware of what was happening to the cinema audience, its simultaneous diminution and fragmentation, as he revealed in an interview for *Alphaville*'s release:

> I really can't see how my films could work [with the public]. I've the impression of doing exactly the opposite of what people want. One can't, with a minimum of consistency, go and see both *Le Gendarme de Saint-Tropez* and *Alphaville* at the same time. Before the war, when Renoir was making *La Bête humaine* and Duvivier was making *Pépé le Moko*, there was still a kind of continuity between the two of them. But today, between Bresson and Verneuil, there's nothing in common.[41]

However successful Godard was in 'killing off' Lemmy Caution in *Alphaville*, the film also announced, in suitably Orphic fashion, a kind of afterlife for him as well. As Larry Gross has argued, there is a direct line of descent from Godard's vision of Constantine as Caution in *Alphaville* to John Borman's portrait of Lee Marvin as Walker in *Point Blank* (1967) and Robert Altman's version of Elliot Gould as Sam Spade in *The Long Goodbye* (1973); each of them is a noir revenant adrift in a world where the villains are either adjuncts to technology or faceless corporate entities.[42] Constantine, too, found an afterlife as much in auteur cinema as in popular cinema, working with R.W. Fassbinder, Agnès Varda, Lars von Trier and with Godard again in *Allemagne 90 neuf zéro* (1991), playing 'the last spy' named Lemmy Caution.

Dystopia discovered and described

> Jeremiah has never had much success in pretending he doesn't thoroughly enjoy his job.
>
> Kingsley Amis, *New Maps of Hell*

The first question to be asked about *Alphaville*'s dystopia is, how seriously should we take it? Was Godard's vision of technological servitude, a talking computer-god and a surveillance-ridden city state already a little derivative, if not old hat, back in the sixties? And isn't the dystopian element in the film just that, an *element*, one among many of which the master collagist avails himself? The answers I propose to these questions are, in reverse order, 'yes', 'yes' and 'very seriously'. Before considering Godard's depiction of dystopia, it's worth recalling how the word has come down to us. As an invented word for an imaginary place, 'dystopia' designates the worst of all possible worlds, but if we consider how familiar the adjective 'dystopian' has become, a shorthand blessing for knee-jerk jeremiahs everywhere, we have to ask: at what point in the long history of 'no places' did the bad begin to edge out the good? The strict meaning of dystopia's antonym 'utopia' is *nowhere* or *no place* but it has often been taken as meaning *good place*, as in the title of Sir Thomas More's classic proposal of an ideal society published in 1516. John Carey describes this as being because of 'confusion of its first syllable with the Greek *eu* as in *euphemism* or *eulogy*. As a result of this mix-up another word *dystopia* has been invented, to mean *bad place*.'[43] The first recorded example of such confusion came on 12 March 1868 (which was a Thursday; a day later and the word would remain minted in fitting irony), when the Radical Member for Westminster, John Stuart Mill, rose in the House of Commons to contribute to the debate on religious equality in the state of Ireland. Mill's words were as follows:

> I may be permitted, as one who, in common with many of my betters, have been subject to the charge of being Utopian, to congratulate the Government on having joined the goodly company. It is, perhaps, too complimentary to call them Utopians, they ought to be called dys-topians, or caco-topians. What is commonly called Utopian is something too good to be practicable; but what they appear to favour is too bad to be practicable.[44]

50 years earlier Jeremy Bentham had employed the term 'cacotopia' in his *Plan of Parliamentary Reform, in the form of a catechism* of 1818: 'As a match for utopia (or the imagined seat of the best government) suppose a cacotopia (or the imagined seat of the worst government) discovered and described.'[45] Few 20th-century writers have sought to retrieve the word 'cacotopia'. In *Nineteen Eighty-Five*, his 'sequel' to George Orwell's *Nineteen Eighty-Four*, Anthony Burgess did not use the word solely for etymological exactness: 'Dystopia has been opposed to eutopia, but both terms come under the utopia heading,' he notes. 'I prefer to call Orwell's imaginary society a cacotopia – on the lines of cacophony or cacodeamon. It sounds worse than dystopia.'[46] Sensibly deciding that 'dystopia' nevertheless remains a 'useful word', Carey makes a useful discrimination:

> Strictly speaking, imaginary good places and imaginary bad places are all utopias, or nowheres ... To count as a utopia, an imaginary place must be an expression of desire. To count as a dystopia, it must be an expression of fear.[47]

The journeys taken through these imaginary places have become a staple of the modern imagination, and Carey is right to describe 'desire' and 'fear' as their impetus. Across the 20th century these journeys have departed from the desire to control the future and to imagine the techniques by which this might be achieved, only to culminate in the fear of having lost control of those same techniques. 'Anyone who had read the literature of utopias during the past two centuries would have had a far better idea of the "shape of things to come" than a newspaper reader who sedulously followed the random reports of events from day to day,' asserted the American writer and architectural historian Lewis Mumford in 1964. 'When collated, the overall design that was taking form throughout society became apparent in these utopias, from a generation to a century in advance.'[48] Writing a few years earlier, the British novelist Kingsley Amis came to a similar conclusion in his 1960 study of science fiction literature, *New Maps of Hell*:

> Whereas 20 years ago, the average yawn-enforcer would locate its authoritarian society on Venus or in the thirtieth century, it would nowadays, I think, set its sights at Earth within the next hundred years or so. The machinery of oppression, then, is wielded not by decadent quasi-aristocrats in ceremonial dress – these are far more common in fantasy – but by business-like managerial types well equipped with the latest technological and psychological techniques for the prevention or detection of heresy.[49]

'Dystopia' really came into its own around the middle of the 20th century, encouraged by a brace of nightmarish fictional speculations that included Yevgeny Zamyatin's *We* (1924), Aldous Huxley's *Brave New World* (1932) and Orwell's *Nineteen Eighty-Four* (1949). Its contemporary coinage was the work of Glen Negley and J. Max Patrick, a pair of American scholars who, in 1952, published *The Quest for Utopia.* In their anthology of imaginary societies, Negley and Patrick described a 17th-century utopian fiction by Joseph Hall, *Mundus Alter et Idem* (*A New World and Yet the Same*, 1605), which they saw as anticipating both Samuel Butler's *Erehwon* (1872) and Huxley's *Brave New World*, as a '*utopia* in the sense of *nowhere*; but it is the opposite of *eutopia*, the ideal society: it is a *dystopia*, if it permissible to coin a word'.[50] Duly coined, the word passed rapidly into common currency, and further studies followed in which the term became firmly established.[51]

Dystopias extrapolate from the present those signs of modernity the promise of which is at best ambiguous and at worse downright frightening, and, in so doing, they hold the idea of 'progress' at an ironic, allegorical distance the better to question it. The dystopian scenario need not be the exclusive preserve of science fiction but, with the genre's propensity for speculation, allegory and straightforward prophecy, it appeared as its natural home. During the 1950s and 1960s a tendency emerges in literature and cinema dramatising a host of fears about the emerging modern landscape, and 'dystopian' becomes its accepted description. As Amis has observed, with science fiction's focus shifting away from depicting other worlds in outer space towards the otherness of life on Earth it was well placed to accommodate the fears that were coalescing at the same moment: fears of automation and atomic destruction, of consumerism and standardisation. Each was a typically modern fear stemming from the suspicion that, beyond modernity's gleaming carapace, behind the windows of skyscraper and department store alike, forces were at work the purpose of which was to control and subjugate humanity. If, by the 1960s, certain conventions were sufficiently well established to be recognised as describing a 'dystopian' vision, then Godard, in *Alphaville*, turns them inside out, inverting them to make them resonate anew.

One can happily travel through *Alphaville* ticking off dystopian tropes – 'tyranny of the machine', 'crime of love', 'visitor from another time', 'city of the future' – which probably explains why, in 1967, Robin Wood claimed,

'In terms of intellectually worked out prophecy, *Alphaville* offers little that is new, most of its ideas about the future of society being traceable to *Nineteen Eighty-Four*, *Brave New World* and other works.'[52] Which is fair, up to a point. Yes, Godard's *Alpha*-ville may well be indebted to Huxley's genetically engineered hierarchy, which runs from alpha to epsilon, just as the all-seeing Alpha 60 can be taken as a surrogate for Orwell's 'Big Brother', but the film also owes something to Zamyatin's depiction of a technocratic autocracy enclosed within a glass city. But, as a low-budget take on *Metropolis* presided over by a high-tech version of Dr Mabuse, *Alphaville* owes equally to Fritz Lang. Wood's criticism neglects Godard's bravura creation of the city itself, not from sets but through filming some of the most modern structures Paris had to offer in 1965 and from the careful selection of surface detail. This undeniably qualifies as much as an 'idea' as a production decision; beyond simply making the most of a limited budget it also observes the 'presence of the future' that was materialising in the metropolitan fabric of Paris. The British novelist J.G. Ballard summed it up well: 'For the first time in science fiction film, Godard makes the point that in the media landscape of the present day the fantasies of science fiction are as "real" as an office block, an airport or a presidential campaign.'[53]

'Silence, logic, security': details of the dystopian city

It is not only the conventional sci-fi image of the futuristic metropolis that Godard invokes in an inverted form (explored more fully in the following section, 'Paris: city of the future') but other conventions as well. The character of Lemmy Caution, for example, is a comical inversion of the 'visitor from another time,' as Godard admitted: 'I didn't imagine society in twenty years from now, as [H.G.] Wells did. On the contrary, I'm telling the story of a man from twenty years ago who discovers the world today and can't believe it.'[54] And it is this man from the past who must confront the 'tyranny of the machine' with the only weapons he has: low cunning, a loaded gun and lyric poetry. Similarly, Lemmy and Natasha join the ranks of characters such as Winston Smith and Julia in *Nineteen Eighty-Four* and D-503 and I-330 in *We* – each guilty of the 'crime of love'. In *Alphaville*, love is not the carnal transgression it is for those other outlaw lovers but a chaste and lyrical romanticism. Love remains a crime, though, because it represents the royal road to the imagination, which allows the lovers to entertain the idea that another world is possible. In the name of 'Silence, logic and security' the avowed purpose of *Alphaville*'s city-state is, bowdlerising Diderot, to strangle the last lover with the entrails of the last poet. One might say that in the eutopian mode all the imagination goes into the world-making, whereas in the dystopian it goes into escaping that world. And, from Zamyatin's *We* – '[Y]ou are sick. And the name of your sickness is FANTASY!' – via *Brave New World*'s bliss-inducing drug Soma to the crowd-pleasing pablum of Prolecult as imagined in *Nineteen Eighty-Four*, the inhabitants of dystopia are everywhere encouraged in their 'eager denial of mind'.[55] The un-policed imagination is the sovereign enemy so, in dystopia, no one will let you dream. There is another dimension to the idea of the no-place worth mentioning. Godard once claimed that the principal achievement of the new wave was to have established a new country on the map of the world and the name of that country was 'cinema'. What could be more utopian than that?

Paris: city of the future

> This was the City, the real City of the Future! For miles and miles and miles, buildings, buildings, buildings. All the same. All lined up. White. Still more

buildings. Buildings, buildings, buildings, buildings, buildings, buildings, buildings, buildings, buildings. Buildings. Buildings.

Christiane Rochefort, *Les Petits Enfants du siècle*[56]

Paris had been Godard's set, playground and Petri dish right from the start, as it was for all the new wave directors shooting their films on location rather than in the studio, as the majority of their predecessors in the French film industry had done. But Godard alone was to explore, doggedly and self-consciously, the city as the laboratory of an emerging civilisation. In this, we can see now, he was taking full advantage of the fortunate congruence of historical circumstances that marked the moment of the French new wave, when modern filmmaking technology met post-war urban modernisation. De Gaulle's return to power was in 1958, and for the next ten years he would preside over post-war recovery, the traumatic twilight of French colonialism in Algeria and increasing economic prosperity. John Ardagh has described this period as being one in which France can be seen to be making 'a leap straight from the late eighteenth to the twentieth century'.[57] The late 1950s and 1960s are therefore transitional years for France, and Paris was where the 'new men' and 'new women' of post-war modernity were emerging to live new lives in new buildings surrounded by the new objects of consumer society. And, of course, they had the new wave of filmmakers to immortalise them, to make them fully 'modern' by giving their images straight back to them. Of all the new wave directors, Godard was the one to do so most avidly, but also with the most evident misgivings about where this modernity was heading. If his subject was cinema and his object modern life in Paris, Godard needed to fuse the two in a new form of cinema, as he admitted in an interview in 1962:

> Cinema, Truffaut said, is spectacle – Méliès – and research – Lumière. If I analyse myself today, I see that I have always wanted, basically, to make a research film in the form of a spectacle. The documentary side is: a man in a particular situation. The spectacle comes when one makes this man a gangster or a secret agent.[58]

The location of *À Bout de souffle* is – with the exception of the opening sequence, shot in Marseilles – Paris, between 17 August and 15 September 1959. As a film in which the action revolves around the Champs Elysées and the streets and cafés of Montmartre, *À Bout de souffle* also provides an image of the city as what one might call an 'elegiac object'. This homage to the city is not only visual; Michel Poiccard (Jean-Paul Belmondo), driving through Paris at night, extols the Haussmann-designed centre to Patricia Francinni (Jean Seberg) with the words 'Look, the Concorde is beautiful', having earlier expressed his dislike of the modern buildings erected across the street from the house of his birth. The building he refers to is a fairly restrained 'international-style' apartment block that coexists comfortably with the 19th-century buildings surrounding it. In the early films of the new wave, the ideal centred city serves to naturalise an image of place that is already iconic: Haussmann's 19th-century centre. This place ('Space in the image of man is place') has become so invested with value by the mid-1960s that filmmakers may turn away from it and exclude it, safe in the knowledge that, even in its absence, it is present as the ancestral, 'elegiac' centre against which the incursions of modern may be measured.[59]

In *Vivre sa vie*, the research side of Godard's work is around the phenomenon of prostitution in the city, the spectacle being Anna Karina as prostitute and the formal organisation of the film into 12 Brechtian-style tableaux. In *Une Femme mariée*, the dominant research element derives from its exploration of a representative new young couple, with the nominal spectacle side coming from the film's sexual intrigue and pop art collage aesthetic. By 1966, with *Deux ou trois choses que je sais d'elle*, the research side starts to dominate, with the focus falling on prostitution in the '*grands ensembles*', a term officially used to describe a housing project containing from 8,000 to 10,000 dwelling units and a population of 30,000 to 40,000. As the historian of Parisian urbanism, Norma Evenson, explains,

> The design of the *grands ensembles* often combined towers and high-rise slabs with five- or six-storey buildings … so rapid was their growth that by 1969 it was estimated that one person in six in the Paris region lived in a *grand ensemble*… As the *grands ensembles* became increasingly dominant in the Paris region, they provided a source of continuing controversy. They were a visible manifestation of the population explosion; the size of the complexes was often overwhelming and the architecture monotonous. It was easy to interpret the *grands ensembles* as a distillation of the worst of modern urban life – to recoil from an environment that seemed to bespeak regimentation and inhuman scale.[60]

Godard's films of the period (like those of Jacques Tati, albeit in a different register) make explicit links between the emerging consumer society, the aesthetic appearance of its structures and objects and the inevitable objectification of its inhabitants. Marie-Claire Ropars-Wuilleumier has pointed out how closely *Alphaville* corresponds to Godard's previous film, *Une Femme mariée*: 'The objects and places of *Alphaville* can easily belong to the same everyday reality as do those of *Une Femme mariée*: they are separated from it by a tone.'[61] The tone of *Une Femme mariée* is quasi-sociological; a young married couple, Charlotte (Macha Méril) and Pierre (Philippe Leroy), live in a newly built Parisian apartment block (the 'Elysée 2' development). He, true to the technocratic form of the time, is an engineer; she is a young mother. It is the exploration of her emotional life, which is divided between her husband and her lover (Bernard Noel), that provides the film's attenuated story, a division mirroring her fragmented existence among the many inducements to consumerism surrounding her. Extending from this is the 'loss of language' that Ropars-Wuilleumier writes about in relation to *Alphaville* and that often happens in Godard's films when characters start to talk in the language of advertising. Pierre, showing off his new television, proudly declares that it is 'aviation technology in the service of television', and the scene will be famously reprised in *Pierrot le fou* when Ferdinand (Jean-Paul Belmondo) attends a party where the guests blather in the tongues of advertising. *Alphaville* is a straightforwardly dystopian vision of technocratic progress, sci-fi noir. Conventionally, science fiction dramatises the question 'What would it be like if … ?' The future is proposed as being latent in the present. *Alphaville* takes the conventional science fiction projection of a dystopian future and says: 'Forget "what if?" Look around you! "If" is already taking place!' The new wave aesthetic of shooting in the streets reaches an apotheosis in *Alphaville*. There is no question of ethnographic realism in the style of Jean Rouch here, nor of the 'neo-realist' approach that the new wave derived from the example of Roberto Rossellini. It is, rather, a short-circuited kind of realism that is applied to the least likely of genres, science fiction, and that serves to make strange a reality that is seen as already being so strange that it positively demands the strategy. To this end, Godard filmed in some of the newest modern structures in Paris, including the Maison de l'ORTF, the headquarters of French national radio and television, which was constructed between 1956 and 1963 and took the form of a circular ring sheathed in glistening metal surrounding a central tower. Other locations included the Esso building in La Défense, the new business district on the western edge of the city that, built between 1958 and 1969, endowed Paris with the monolithic corporate skyline of a 20th-century world city. In addition, we are given a glimpse of the high-rise housing blocks of the *grands ensembles* known as HLMs ('Habitations à loyer modéré', or low-rent housing), sardonically recast by the film as 'hôpitaux de la longue maladie', re-education centres for the misfits of Alphaville.

By 1965 the modern city, its interiors and outskirts had come to be associated with the particular aesthetic characteristics of obsessive geometry and standardising design, and with these aesthetic marks of the modern came accompanying judgements concerning alienation, isolation and automation. By the time of *Alphaville*, the modern city is uniformly associated with a dystopian image that gets progressively worse the further away the camera moves from the ancestral centre. *Deux ou trois choses que je sais d'elle*, shot in the *grands ensembles* of La Courneuve, was inspired, according to Godard, 'by a letter in *Le Nouvel Observateur* from a woman reader replying to an inquiry into part-time prostitution in the new high-rise housing developments'.[62] Pierre Sorlin, writing on the relationship between the character Juliette Janson (Marina Vlady) in *Deux ou trois choses* and her environment, suggests that, 'by separating the life of Juliette from the city in which she lives', Godard 'emphasized the artificiality of the story. The outer setting, the city, becomes thus an independent part of the narrative, almost an autonomous character.'[63] Given that the film's subtitle is 'Elle: la région parisienne' it's hard to disagree with Sorlin, but he overemphasises the autonomy of the city's image in the film. This image is no longer simply 'background' or 'setting' but is integrated into a highly reflexive documentary-style investigation into the phenomenon known as 'la sarcellite'. This journalistic designation (named after Sarcelles, one of the largest of such housing developments) was coined to describe the malign effects of living in the *grands ensembles*, here incarnated in a young woman who turns to part-time prostitution in order to makes ends meet. The processes of objectification crucial to consumer society are shown here at their most extreme, wherein a young woman must sell herself as an object in order to afford other objects. Where it might previously have been possible to talk about an ideal image of the city that presumed harmony between character and environment, a favourable integration, in *Deux ou trois choses* we are presented with an image of an entirely different order. Juliette is not physically

Alphaville: the tell-tale signs of a non-place

integrated into the city where she lives but into a circuit of economic demands and desires that the *grands ensembles* come to represent: an image of dystopian integration, of dis-integration. The prostitute – a stock figure of Parisian mythology from Baudelaire and Impressionist painting onwards – returns as false consciousness made flesh. The film ends with a series of consumer items – boxes of washing powder, transistor radios – lined up in a rectilinear replication of the layout of the *grands ensembles.* Under Godard's camera, these objects offer the economic relations behind the suburban new towns as metonymic of consumer society: boxes, boxes, boxes standing in for buildings, buildings, buildings.

From no-place to non-place

> We know that Benjamin's interest in Parisian passages and, more generally, in iron and glass architecture, stems partly from the fact that he sees these things as embodying a wish to prefigure the architecture of the next century, as a dream of anticipation. By the same token, we may wonder whether yesterday's representatives of modernity, who found material for reflection in the world's concrete space, might not have illuminated in advance certain

aspects of today's supermodernity; not through the accident of a few lucky intuitions, but because they already embodied in an exceptional way (because they were artists) situations (postures, attitudes) which, in more prosaic form, have now become the common lot.

Marc Augé, *Non-Places: Introduction to an Anthropology of Supermodernity*[64]

'Architecture in film is never just itself,' warns Peter Wollen, and this is especially true of *Alphaville*. Drawing on the work of the French ethnographer Marc Augé, Wollen considers how his idea of space in the contemporary world as dividing into 'place' and 'non-place' might be applied to cinema.[65] According to Augé, the non-place is transitional space such as one finds in airports, service stations, supermarkets and hotels. These are spaces devoid of ancestral features, historical associations and private meanings – all the things that combine to give 'space' a sense of 'place'. Non-place is full of signs, instructions, advertising and images. Non-place serenades the stroller with piped mood music. Non-place is the future of what Augé calls 'super modernity'. Of course, there is no such thing as a non-place, in the way that Augé defines it, in cinema. Filmed space has a function, helping to construct the narrative space of the film while also drawing on and developing a host of other associations. A bedroom is never simply a place for sleeping in, a staircase never just a way of going up or down stairs, a corridor never simply a matter of a receding perspective. Wollen makes a distinction between the space created by the production designer, essentially 'a static space', and the space created by the cinematographer and editor, which is 'a dynamic, narrative space'.[66] *Alphaville* is almost entirely made up of architectural non-places: the city is a patchwork of transitional zones – corridors, staircases, offices, hotel rooms – liberally interspersed with their characteristic signage – arrows, numbers, neon (an aspect of the film's 'afterlife', which I explore in the final chapter). But the narrative space that Godard sculpts from details abstracted from the built environment is a labyrinth, warped and uncanny. Lemmy's hotel room might appear to be one of the relatively few settled spaces in the film and this is partly because of its generic associations, as Harun Farocki has observed:

The hotel room is an important location in detective fiction – an anonymous place for love, a drink, a suicide. Lemmy's room is no exception. It is the site, in quick succession of seduction, violence and romance. Lemmy has no

> sooner disposed of an intruder and an unwanted woman than the ravishing Natasha von Braun makes her dramatic appearance.[67]

But the space of this room is curiously elastic (see Appendix 1, Sequence 1). Two doors lead to a bathroom, which allows the characters to circulate without the camera following them. Given the amount of time we spend with Lemmy in his hotel room, it is surprising how little we actually see of the bathroom, which rather lends it the quality of an imaginary space. While its dimensions seem to be revealed briefly during the early fight sequence it is nevertheless associated with the cop's initial mysterious appearance as a disembodied voice. The jukebox that sits incongruously in the corner dispensing soporific mood music (a further tell-tale sign of the non-place) is surely present to emphasise the strangeness of this room. From the film's outset, with Paris transformed into Alphaville and the present into the future, Godard alerts us that space and time are both to be made strange.

Notes

1 Faiola, Anthony, 'Brazil's elites fly above their fears: rich try to wall off urban violence', *Washington Post Foreign Service*, 1 June 2002.
2 Ibid.
3 Fishman, Robert, *Global Suburbs* paper presented to the First Biennial Conference of the Urban Historical Association, Pittsburgh, September 2002.
4 Ibid.
5 *Viver a Vida Alphaville: Alphaville 30 anos* (Mauro Ivan Marketing editorial, São Paulo, 2003), pp. 216–217.
6 Amengual, Barthélemy, *Bande à part de Jean-Luc Godard* (Éditions Yellow Now, Belgium, 1993), pp. 131–132.
7 Wake, Sandra and Hayden, Nicola, *Bonnie and Clyde* (Lorrimer, London, 1972), p. 23.
8 Ibid. pp. 23–24.
9 Ibid. pp. 23–24.
10 Interview with Raoul Coutard, Nanterre, 18 November 2003.
11 From author's correspondence with Charles Bitsch, April 2004 (translated by CD).
12 Bergala, Alain (ed.), *Jean-Luc Godard par Jean-Luc Godard*, vol. 1, *1950–1984* (Cahiers du cinéma, Paris, 1998), p. 254.
13 Cerisuelo, Marc, *Jean-Luc Godard* (Éditions des Quatre-Vents, Paris, 1989), p. 109.
14 Ibid. p. 109.
15 Godard's description of *Une Femme est une femme* was given in a lengthy interview with *Cahiers du cinéma*: 'Entretien: les *Cahiers* rencontrent Godard après ses quatre premiers films', 138, 1962, in Bergala (ed.), *Jean-Luc Godard par*

Jean-Luc Godard, vol. 1, p. 224. Godard described Paul Javal as 'a character from *Marienbad* who wants to play the role of a character from *Rio Bravo*' in 'Scénario du *Mépris*: ouverture', *Cahiers du cinéma* 146, 1963 in Bergala (ed.), *Jean-Luc Godard par Jean-Luc Godard*, vol. 1, p. 243.

16 MacCabe, Colin, *Godard: Images, Sounds, Politics* (British Film Institute and Macmillan, London, 1980), p. 160.

17 Interview with Jackie Reynal, *Cahiers du cinéma* 'Spécial Godard: 30 ans depuis', November 1990, p. 25.

18 Ibid. p. 25.

19 Interview with Raoul Coutard.

20 National Film Theatre, Akim Tamiroff programme (undated).

21 The story of Welles' ill-fated production of *Don Quixote* reveals a connection between the careers of Tamiroff and his co-star in *Alphaville*, Howard Vernon. Vernon worked frequently with the Spanish pulp-horror director Jesus Franco, who, in 1992, released a controversial assembly of the footage Welles had shot of Cervantes' tale under the title *Don Quixote de Orson Welles.*

22 'Howard Vernon: d'Orlaf à Hermocrate', *Cahiers du cinéma* 505, 1996, p. 8.

23 Anna Karina interviewed by Colin MacCabe, National Film Theatre, London, June 2001.

24 Jackson, Kevin, 'The divine Miss K gets real', *The Independent*, 29 June 2001.

25 Atkinson, Michael, 'Anna Karina's magnificent movieness', *Village Voice*, 15 August 2001.

26 Farber, Manny, 'Jean-Luc Godard', in M. Farber, *Negative Space: Manny Farber on the Movies* (Da Capo Press, New York, 1998), p. 266.

27 'Entretien avec Eddie Constantine', *Cinématographe* 63, 1980.

28 Godard claimed that it had been been Constantine's wish to make a vampire film. *Les Nouvelles Littéraires*, 1 April 1965.

29 *La Paresse* exists online in the form of a *photo-roman* at http://www.chez.com/alaincine3/Godard/61Peches.htm.

30 Godard had also talked about Belmondo in *À Bout de souffle* in similar terms: 'I saw him as a kind of block that it was necessary to film in order to discover what was behind it.' In Marie, Michel, *À Bout de souffle étude critique* (Éditions Nathan, Paris, 1999), p. 104. When discussing working with Alain Delon on his 1990 film *Nouvelle Vague*, Godard referred to filming him 'as if he was a tree'.

31 *Cinématographe* 63, 1980.

32 Jacob, Gilles, 'Alphaville: un cauchemar non climatisé', *Cinéma* 65, 1965, p. 116.

33 Wenders, Wim, 'New hat, same old scars: Eddie Constantine' in W. Wenders, *Emotion Pictures: Reflections on the Cinema*, translated by S. Whiteside and M. Hoffman (Faber and Faber, London, 1986), p. 69.

34 Interview with Raoul Coutard.

35 *Cinématographe* 63, 1980.

36 Ibid.

37 Elkaïm, Arlette, 'Alphaville ou Bétafilm?', *Les Temps Modernes* 229, 1965, p. 2293.

38 Godard, Jean-Luc, *Arts* 713, 1959, and 'L'Afrique vous parle de la fin et des moyens', *Cahiers du cinéma* 94, 1959, in Bergala (ed.), *Jean-Luc Godard par Jean-Luc Godard*, vol. 1, p. 182.

39 Bergala (ed.), *Jean-Luc Godard par Jean-Luc Godard*, vol. 1, pp. 181–182.

40 *Hollywood Reporter*, 23 September 1977, p. 12.

41 Godard is commenting on the division, as he saw it, between the 'popular' and '*cinéphile*' audiences that developed between the 1930s – when Julien Duvivier made *Pépé le Moko* (1937) and Jean Renoir, a key auteur director, made *La Bête humaine* (1938), both starring the leading male star of the period, Jean Gabin – and the 1960s. The film he positions in polar opposition to *Alphaville, Le Gendarme de Saint-Tropez* (Jean Girault, 1964), was a vehicle for the popular French comedian Louis de Funes. Godard further exemplifies this division with reference to Henri Verneuil, the director of mainstream films such as *Des gens sans importance* (1955) and *Mélodie en sous sol* (1963), and Robert Bresson, the auteur director of *Pickpocket* (1959) and *Au Hasard, Balthazar* (1966). *Paris-presse,* 12 May 1965.
42 Gross, Larry, 'Film après noir', *Film Quarterly,* July–August 1976, pp. 44–49.
43 Carey, John, *The Faber Book of Utopias* (Faber and Faber, London, 1999), p. xi.
44 *Hansard,* 12 March 1868, 1517/1.
45 Bentham, Jeremy, *Plan of Parliamentary Reform, in the form of a catechism* (T.J. Wooler, London, 1818). The stem of *cacotopia* derives from the Greek word *kakos* meaning 'bad', as in *cacophony*: in referring to Bentham's coinage, Mill was paying homage to the man who had been his mentor and teacher in the theory of Utilitarianism and who also endowed our present-day dystopias with one of their most powerful defining symbols, the perfect 'rational' system of surveillance known as the 'Panopticon'.
46 Mumford, Lewis, *The Myth of the Machine: The Pentagon of Power* (Secker and Warburg, London, 1964), p. 220; Burgess, Anthony, *Nineteen Eighty-Five* (Arrow Books, London, 1980), p. 52.
47 Carey, *The Faber Book of Utopias,* p. xi.
48 Mumford, *The Myth of the Machine,* pp. 212–213.
49 Amis, Kingsley, *New Maps of Hell* (Victor Gollancz, London, 1960), p. 84.
50 Negley, Glen and Patrick, J. Max, *The Quest for Utopia: An Anthology of Imaginary Societies* (McGrath Publishing Company, College Park, MD, 1971), p. 298.
51 See Walsh, Chad, *From Utopia to Nightmare* (Geoffrey Bles, London, 1962); Hillegas, Mark R., *The Future as Nightmare: H.G. Wells and the Anti-utopians* (Oxford University Press, New York, 1967); Sontag, Susan, 'The imagination of disaster', in S. Sontag, *Against Interpretation and Other Essays* (Farrar, Strauss and Giroux, New York, 1968).
52 Wood, Robin, '*Alphaville*', in I. Cameron (ed.), *The Films of Jean-Luc Godard* (Studio Vista, London, 1967), p. 83.
53 Ballard, J.G., *A User's Guide to the Millennium* (HarperCollins, London, 1996), p. 19.
54 Baby, Yvonne, 'Dresser des embuscades dans le planification: entretien avec Jean-Luc Godard', *Le Monde,* 6 May 1965.
55 Amis, *New Maps of Hell,* p. 96.
56 Rochefort, Christiane, *Les petits enfants du siècle* (Grasset, Paris, 1961), pp. 124–125.
57 Ardagh, John, *The New French Revolution: A Social and Economic Survey of France 1945–1967* (Secker and Warburg, London, 1968), p. 9.
58 Godard, 'Entretien', p. 223.
59 Aldo Van Eyck, Dutch architect and member of the architectural collective Team Ten, gives this idealist conception of 'space' and 'place' in Jencks, Charles, *Modern Movements in Architecture* (Penguin, London and New York, 1973), p. 311.

60 Evenson, Norma, *Paris: A Century of Change, 1878–1978* (Yale University Press, New Haven, CT and London, 1979), pp. 239–240.
61 Ropars-Wuilleumier, Marie-Claire, 'Loss of language', *Wide Angle* 1 (3), 1976, translated by Dorothea Hockzema, p. 19.
62 Godard, Jean-Luc, '*One or Two Things*: Jean-Luc Godard', *Sight and Sound*, Winter 1966/1967, p. 4.
63 Sorlin, Pierre, *European Cinemas and European Societies 1939–1990* (Routledge, London, 1991), p. 133.
64 Augé, Marc, *Non-Places: Introduction to an Anthropology of Supermodernity*, translated by J. Howe (Verso, London and New York, 1995), pp. 93–94.
65 Wollen, Peter, 'Architecture and Film: Places and Non-Places', in P. Wollen, *Paris Hollywood: Writings on Film* (Verso, London and New York, 2002), pp. 199–215.
66 Ibid. p. 202.
67 Silverman, Kaja and Farocki, Harun, '*Alphaville*: words like love', in K. Silverman and H. Farocki, *Speaking About Godard* (New York University Press, New York, 1998), p. 62.

2 The shape of things

Light that goes…

Lemmy Caution's light sabre

Alpha 60: What transforms night into day?

Lemmy Caution: Poetry.

In a 1965 interview with *Le Monde* Godard stated, 'We shot at night because night means adventure and romance. And also because it's a film about light.'[1] Which is a bit like a writer describing a novel as being 'about' words or a painter saying a painting is 'about' paint. The phrase is reassuringly Godardian, a statement of the ontologically obvious that, on examination, reveals the paradox that illuminates it. How can any film shot on celluloid and projected in a cinema *not* be 'about' light? In the cinema, after all, we inhabit the realms of light and darkness simultaneously. Or, as Chris Marker has put it,

> Godard nailed it once and for all: at the cinema you raise your eyes to the screen; in front of the television you lower them. Then there is the role of the shutter. Out of the two hours you spend in a movie theatre, you spend one of them in the dark. It's this nocturnal portion that stays with us, that fixes our memory of a film in a different way to the same film seen on television or on a monitor.[2]

One could start here and proceed to read *Alphaville* as an allegory of cinematic light. Its opening image of a glaring, screen-sized bulb beams right back into the projector bringing the image to the screen and, flashing on and off, alerts us to the opposite of its cruel brilliance: the darkness by which it needs to be perceived to do its work of illumination. 'The light flashes according to some pattern or code unfamiliar to us,' Gilberto Perez has suggested:

> This is a signifying light, as always at the movies, but here the messages it transmits are not to be readily readable ... Laying bare, in this movie about the machine society, the material elements of his machine medium and the way it produces sights and sounds, Godard hints at a connection between the movie's author and the sovereign machine that its fiction erects as the villain.[3]

In other words, it's a gesture of mischievous cosmogony. Godard said: 'Let there be Light.' And there was light, and he saw that it was good. And the voice of God was that of a computer (actually, a man with a mechanical voice box replacing his cancer-damaged larynx) with an opening declaration that is both God-like and like Godard, and has a fairy-tale familiarity to it.[4] Alpha 60's declaration that 'there are times when reality becomes too complex for oral communication' does the work of 'once upon a time', and the oracular pronouncement that 'legend gives it a form by which it pervades the whole world' promises that the modern world is to be explored according to the imperatives of myth. As a film 'about light' shot mostly at night, *Alphaville* will be as much about shadows as luminescence, as much about black as white, and, after all, there is no shortage of mythical possibilities that take shape around the idea, and the ideal, of light.

From *À Bout de souffle* onwards, Godard had insisted on a commitment to filming in natural light and to the experience of location shooting as opposed to the artificial light of the studio environment. In this, one could say that he was asserting his new wave credentials. Central to the perceived shock and novelty of new wave cinema was the fact that its filmmakers shot in the streets of Paris, filming on location with small crews. Raoul Coutard recalled Godard's words to him when they were preparing *À Bout de souffle*: 'No more confectionery. We're going to shoot in real light.'[5] *Alphaville* is closely related to Godard's debut, not so much in its attachment to the pursuit of 'real light' (for all its blizzards of artificial light *Alphaville* is a film shot in 'real darkness') but in terms of developing the lighting and camera techniques previously essayed in the night-time sequences that Coutard had shot for *À Bout de souffle*. A legend that has built up around that film can be laid to rest at this point and *Alphaville* provides the opportunity to correct and clarify the technical detail that has contributed to it. As recently as Colin MacCabe's biographical portrait of Godard, published in 2003, the claim persists that, for the night shoots on *À Bout de souffle*, the use of a film stock that was manufactured only for still photography required the crew 'to stick together as many rolls of 17.5 metres as would make up a magazine of film'. Michel Marie, author of a shot-by-shot study of the film, has also stated that this was the case.[6] Coutard, however, insists that it is self-evidently false to claim that the stock was stuck together in this fashion. As he puts it:

> You'd see the adhesive in the image! No, we used whole lengths. If we had 10 metres of film we'd do a take of 20 seconds, for example. We had two or three lengths of 60 metres, that's to say 2 minutes of film, and some of 40 metres which makes 80 seconds of film, and also some lengths of 20 and 10 metres. We bought everything in Paris that Ilford had of that particular film stock. When we had to do a close-up we used a length of 10 metres, 20 seconds, and we had our close-up. The advantage of the Éclair Cameflex is that it's very quick to load, so we loaded magazines with different lengths of film.[7]

This might seem an unnecessarily pedantic clarification of a minor technical detail, but it was because such film stock no longer needed to be used in small quantities that the particular, high-contrast black and white look of *Alphaville* was technically possible. By the time that Godard and Coutard came to shoot the film, Ilford had started to manufacture its HPS stock for film cameras as well. A further technical aspect links *Alphaville* with *À Bout de souffle*: the exploration of film development processes. But this insistence on pushing technical boundaries, shooting mostly at night with minimal but intense lighting on highly sensitive film stock, was not without its problems.

> When we developed the film for [the night-time sequences in] *À Bout de souffle*, the laboratory in France only offered a small machine that was used for test reels. With *Alphaville* we had to use a much larger machine since it was going to have to process a whole film. The French labs didn't want to put a single machine at our disposal for the film, so we had it developed in London at Humphreys Laboratory. There was a major technical problem with this film stock, though. When it was sent to London it was subjected to a lot of movement and vibration because it was being transported by car and aeroplane and we had problems with static electricity. The strips of film would rub against each other in transit and when they were unspooled they could release sparks that would mark the negative so that we couldn't use it. We had enormous problems because of this, so we were obliged to do certain scenes four times over, to get four good takes in order to be sure not to have this problem. Because we had to wait two days to know whether we had any problems we were obliged for the sake of security to do four good takes.[8]

Alphaville, then, originates in the night of *À Bout de souffle*, but the cafés and boulevards of ancestral Paris are replaced by neon-lit, curtain-walled monoliths shrouded in Expressionist shadows. It is not only the technical innovations of its cinematography and lighting that makes *Alphaville* a 'film about light'. It is so because light is both the substance and theme of the film and is treated on many levels. Pushed to extremes of luminosity and shadow, its black and white film summons forth from the history of cinema the 'haunted' light of German Expressionism and film noir. But the spectrum of light motifs from which Godard draws is wider than just film-historical. City of Light and home to those 'brothers-in-light' who 'invented' cinema, les frères Lumières, Paris is transformed into Alphaville, City of Night and Capital of Pain, a nocturnal technocracy illuminated by a post-atomic brilliance burning more brightly than a thousand suns. Our guide to this overlit underworld is Lemmy Caution, Orpheus in a trenchcoat. 'Lemmy is a character who carries light to people who no longer know what it is', was how Godard described Constantine's role.[9] The inhabitants of Alphaville depend on electricity for their survival, but, as Kaja Silverman has observed, '[T]hey have forgotten the sacred origins of light. With his cigarette lighter, Lemmy seeks to reignite their memories. He is Prometheus once again carrying fire from the gods to humanity.'[10] The evidence is there from the moment we first glimpse Lemmy, sitting in the darkness of his car (see Appendix 1, Sequence 1). His face is momentarily lit up beneath his hat by the cigarette lighter he snaps open, producing a simple flame that burns, briefly and brightly, in direct challenge to the tyrannical glare pulsing under the voice of Alpha 60, that of an interrogator's angle poise, a prison-camp arc light. Driving a white Ford Galaxy, wearing a white overcoat and carrying a white briefcase, Lemmy arrives in Alphaville *armed* with light, and, to reinforce the point, Lemmy examines his pistol having lit his cigarette. Among the weapons he carries are his camera, with a flash that sometimes bleaches out the image, and his lighter which also comes in handy when he first encounters Natasha von Braun.

Natasha's entrance is given something of a build-up (see Appendix 1, Sequences 1 and 2). After despatching an Alphaville enforcer who has appeared in his bathroom from nowhere, Lemmy takes a few snaps of Béatrice, the Third Class *séductrice* who has escorted him to his room, when the omnipresent voice of Alpha 60 informs him that 'Miss Natasha von Braun' is waiting for him in the lobby. What follows is handled with pace and economy and is full of significant details. Speaking into what looks like a bedside alarm clock, Lemmy replies that he'll be down in five minutes only to be informed that Natasha is already on her way up. Taking out his notebook, Lemmy extracts two photographs. One of them shows a stern-looking man in horn-rimmed spectacles, Professor von Braun, Natasha's father. As he consults the notes written on the back of each portrait, Lemmy murmurs Natasha's name. The other photograph shows a more grizzled individual, Lemmy's fellow secret agent, Henry Dickson. A certain amount of necessary plot exposition is thus swiftly dealt with: two important characters are introduced as another is about to arrive on the scene. But, before she does, Lemmy needs to prepare for her arrival, which he does by indulging in a spot of target practice. Placing his cigarette lighter on top of the TV set he whips a pistol out of his suitcase and shoots, igniting its flame. From this point on in the scene a wealth of light motifs are introduced, marking and, in many ways, defining the relationship between Lemmy and Natasha. The flash and report of Lemmy's gun cover the cut to the shot of the lighter aflame, and we hear the first stirrings of Natasha's musical theme and then her voice for the first time as she asks: 'Have you got a light?' Leaning in the doorway of his hotel room, as languidly provocative as Lauren

Bacall when she first meets Humphrey Bogart in *To Have and Have Not* (Howard Hawks, 1944), Natasha's words to Lemmy are a fond parody of Bacall's request of Bogart: 'Anyone got a match?' 'Yeah,' Lemmy replies, as he brings his flame to her cigarette, 'I came 9,000 kilometres to give it to you.'

Thus we are introduced to Natasha as we were to Lemmy, through the lighting of a cigarette. In classical Hollywood cinema the simple gesture of a man lighting a woman's cigarette comes charged with the suggestive spark of smouldering intensity and sexual intimacy. Here, the exchange, while carrying some sexual connotations, symbolises the start of Natasha's awakening from the narcotic slumber of life in Alphaville. As she raises the cigarette to her lips to accept the light from Lemmy, Natasha stands in the darkened doorway of his room and moves slightly towards the left of the frame which is bisected, half in darkness, half in light. She moves away from darkness towards the light and this movement will come to define her journey throughout the film. As Harun Farocki has observed, these two shots – of the cigarette lighter and of Natasha in the doorway – further expand 'the semantic range of the word "light" or, in the French, "feu" ("fire")'.[11] A creature but not a native of Alphaville, Natasha is unfamiliar with the light (let alone the word) of 'love' that Lemmy has carried to her

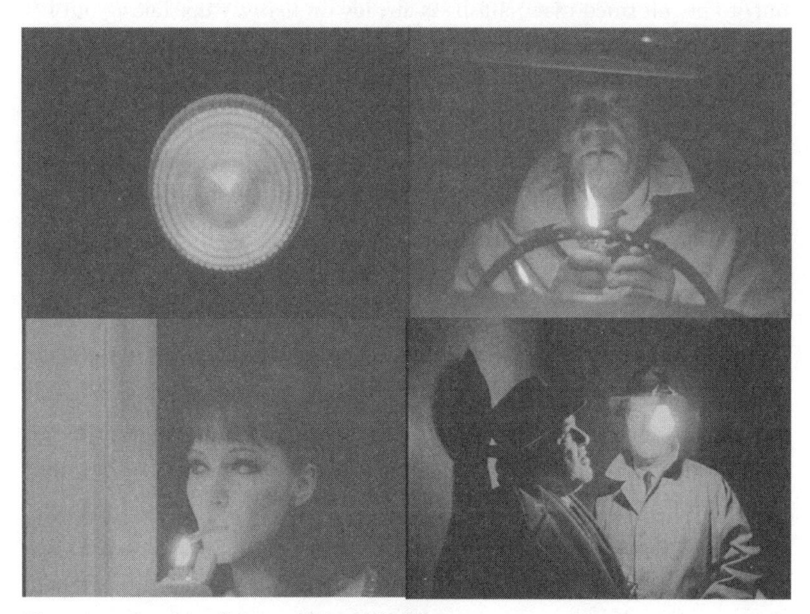

Fire versus electricity: light motifs in *Alphaville*

across 'intersidereal space'. Drawn to it, she has no name for it and so pulls away. Yet there are strong suggestions that the two of them are destined to meet and fall in love. Consider, for example, how Natasha is already on her way to Lemmy's room as he prepares to meet her in the lobby; how Lemmy's laconic one-liner about coming 9,000 kilometres to give her a light is a declaration of the film's story; and how, when she tells Lemmy: 'My name is Natasha von Braun,' he replies: 'I know.' 'How do you know?' she asks. There are, as Lemmy Caution might put it, some things you just *know*. Later, he will observe that 'Natasha is a name from the past', only for her to respond with the Alphaville mantra that 'you can only know what exists in the present. No-one has lived in the past and no one can live in the future.' But Lemmy must deal with Natasha as she is, hesitant and vacillating, full of uncertain ardour, hovering between two states: the overlit somnolence of her place in Alphaville as a 'Second Class Programmer' and the interior illumination of her heart that Lemmy promises.

However, it is not only what we *see* that describes Natasha's uncertain progress from the dark light of Alphaville towards the illumination of love but also what we *hear*. Sound has a particular significance when one considers the role that language plays in the film, whether in the form of the forbidden words that are erased daily from the Alphaville dictionary or in the lyrical force of poetry, not to mention the strange inverted speech of the city's inhabitants. The rhythm and pitch of Natasha's voice modulates and shifts throughout this scene, from girlish gaiety to sombre intonation, from an auditory 'light' to 'dark'. Sitting in the same chair where Béatrice preened while Lemmy took her photograph, Natasha's manner of speaking changes in the space of a few sentences from lively and animated ('…completement idiote!') to slower and sadder ('Oui, Monsieur Johnson … réception spectacle'), as though she were at first trying to escape from and then succumbs to the sleepwalker's whisper of Alphaville-speak. But in the same sequence, at the same moment, Godard emphasises something else that participates as fully in the range of light and dark motifs as does the luminescence (or otherwise) of the image and the emphasis on the voice: the look of one character to the other. As Natasha sits, intoning gravely about the 'réception spectacle' to which Lemmy is invited, she lowers her eyes and the camera moves slowly round to reframe her head-on. Having established the frontal framing in which both Natasha and then Lemmy are shot, Godard cuts in closer still to Karina, her large dark eyes, emphasised by her make-up, now raised to Lemmy. Such frontal shots carry a certain charge familiar from other early Godard films. From the sequence in *À Bout de souffle* when Belmondo turns to the camera and nonchalantly informs those spectators who 'don't love the countryside, the seaside or the mountains' that they can 'piss off', to the sequences in *La Chinoise* (1967) where members of a Parisian sect of Maoist students recite passages from the Little Red Book, Godard's repeated recourse to such frontal framing accrues different connotations across his career. Film theory has conventionally turned to Brecht's idea of 'the alienation effect', which, although it was developed in relation to theatrical conventions, has been used to consider Godard's use of frontal framing as breaking the so-called 'fourth wall' of cinematic identification by having a character look directly at the audience, addressing them in such a way as, supposedly, to preclude or undercut the spectator's identification with the character. While this may well be the case in a film such as *La Chinoise*, it is not, or not exclusively so, in earlier examples of Godard's use of such framing. Two cases in particular can be called upon to illuminate its first appearance in *Alphaville*.

In *Vivre sa vie*, Karina plays Nana, a young Parisian shop girl who, because of a debt, loses her flat, falls into prostitution and is killed by a pimp. At one point in the film Nana visits a cinema, where she watches Dreyer's *La Passion de Jeanne d'Arc/The Passion of Joan of Arc* (1928), and the vision of Maria Falconetti as Joan reduces her to tears. Godard films this sequence in a series of shot/counter-shots that alternate between images from Dreyer's film and frontal, close-up shots of Karina with her eyes welling. Several correspondences between the world of Godard's filmmaking and that of Dreyer's are exploited here; some of them are formal while others reside more in the realm of biography or anecdote but are significant nonetheless. Like Dreyer, Karina is Danish by birth, and her mother was a costume designer on the director's *Gertrud* (1964);[12] biographical correspondences that Godard explicitly acknowledged when he named the first character that Karina was to play for him, in *Le petit soldat*, Véronique Dreyer. The frontal framing that Godard exploits in his image of Nana's overwhelming feeling of identification with Falconetti draws its associative power directly from Dreyer's obsessive concentration on his actress's face, which reveals, as Jacques Aumont puts it, 'the face of the soul'.[13] What we have here, then, are a couple of 'holy whores': one of them on-screen (a further biographical detail thickens the tragic texture of this scene when one learns that Falconetti herself came to a miserable end as a prostitute) and the other weeping at her vision in the stalls. Perez is right to describe the 'star selfhood' that Karina assumed with Godard as being 'an emblem of the soul, a signifier of tenderness, a concrete manifestation of unsuppressible beauty and humanity'.[14] Karina is linked to Falconetti by Godard's recourse to the frontal framing of a woman's face to call forth the idea of the soul, the reference to which runs throughout the film as the corollary to the theme of prostitution. *Vivre sa vie* is, as Godard described it, 'the story of a woman who sells her body while keeping her soul', and, at the end of the first of the 12 'tableaux' that make up the film's structure, Paul (André Labarthe) tells Nana a children's story. As he recites the story, his voice is removed from the ambience of the café where the scene takes place to become more intimate. 'La poule,' Paul narrates ('poule' means 'chicken' in French but is also a slang term for 'a bird' or 'a chick') 'is a creature made up of an interior, and an exterior. If you remove the exterior, you'll find the interior and when you take away the interior there you find the soul.' Ginette Vincendeau has observed how, in *Vivre sa vie* and in Godard's other films

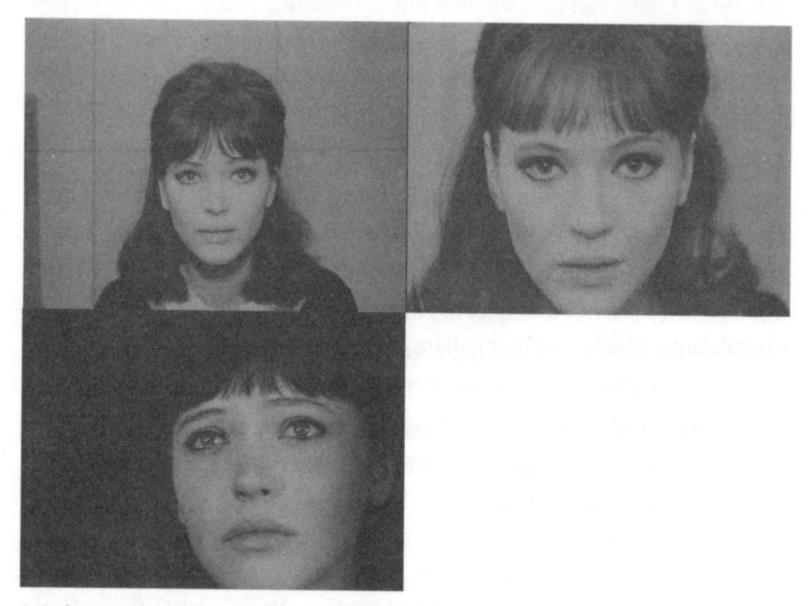

Windows to the soul: Anna Karina, frontally framed, in *Alphaville* and *Vivre sa vie*

with Karina, it is the 'Pygmalion'-like relationship between the director and his actress that is on display:

> In section XII of *Vivre sa vie*, pages from Edgar Allan Poe's *The Oval Portrait* are read to Nana by the male character who is in love with her, dubbed with Godard's voice. *The Oval Portrait* (the story of a painter so in love with the portrait of his lover that he neglects the real woman, who dies) provides the 'poetic' justification for Nana's death where the film's motivation is weak and arbitrary, highlighting the fact that we are watching a story between director and actress rather than between two characters.[15]

In *Le petit soldat*, when the principal character Bruno Forestier (Michel Subor) is taking photographs of Véronique Dreyer he observes: 'When one photographs a face, one photographs the soul behind it.' What is evident in both films, though, is that the 'soul' reveals itself through the mediation of either photography or cinema. It is the presence of these in both scenes that provides an alibi for Godard's frontal framing, whether in the shot/counter-shot exchange of Nana in the cinema and Falconetti on the screen or Véronique before the camera and Bruno behind it. In *Alphaville*, however, this moment of frontal framing has no obvious mediation by which to summon forth the idea of 'the soul', which is whatever the all-seeing, all-knowing Alpha 60 cannot grasp of Natasha, that which lies 'behind the face' and must be eliminated in the time-honoured way of every dystopia worthy of the name. In this sequence, it is what we *cannot* see that counts: the secret exchange of the light of love between a man and a woman. Just as this cannot be seen, nor can it be spoken of, and the theme of the soul's illumination by love will be further developed in the references to poetry as an analogous, forbidden form of illumination in which the words of love combine with the look of love, the ardent eye and the lyric voice united against Alpha 60's eye and voice of power. Another of the film's organising motifs, the line, comes into play here, and goes some way to explaining the force of these frontal shots, which is further enhanced by the complete absence in the film of anything approaching a conventional shot/counter-shot exchange. In the neon arrows that flash onto the screen or in the corridors where the tunnelling perspective is emphasised by the camera's implacably linear movement, the forms of the line and the circle vie with each other throughout the film. The line also features as a spoken image of aspiration and intention delivered by characters in the film. Natasha hears an Alphaville dissident who, on the point of being 'liquidated', exclaims: 'In order to create life, it is merely necessary to advance in a straight line towards all that we love.' Later, in the remarkably lyrical love scene, she recites, 'We must advance to live. Aim straight ahead towards those you love. I went towards you. I went endlessly towards the light.' And, as if to prefigure her transformation in that scene, Godard shoots Natasha and Lemmy frontally, looking along a line of extramission that runs straight from eye to eye. Later, in a prelude to the love scene, Natasha is again filmed in an almost identical combination of camera movement and frontal framing. In this film 'about light', how could the eye – as a window on the world and mirror of the soul – not be privileged? Eye, window, mirror: in the radiant city of Alphaville nothing is allowed to go unseen and optical surrogates abound; a window is either a glaring compound eye of oppressively bright facets, or an opaque mirror full of reflections that gives onto nothing beyond itself. But it is also the portal to another knowledge, another world, and to the birth of Natasha's interior life, to '*la conscience*'.

However, at this stage in the film, Natasha is only dimly aware of the journey she is on, troubled by this stranger's gaze and awakening to something she cannot name. As she and Lemmy leave his hotel room to walk down the corridor to the lift, their mutual incomprehension is made clear (see Appendix 1, Sequence 2). Tracking back in a single take, the camera moves ahead of the couple as they walk. Natasha wears an item of clothing that is a virtual insignia of her uncertain position between light and darkness, a knee-length coat that is entirely black except for an extravagant white circular trim at its hem, which creeps up the coat's front. Lemmy, having donned his white mac, answers her questions about his life in the Outerlands but soon finds their conversation frustrating. As they move in and out of the pools of light that dapple the corridor, the conversation becomes increasingly fraught with incomprehension. 'No one ever falls in love with you?' Lemmy asks her in astonishment when they discuss her job of entertaining visitors to the city. 'In love? What's that?' Natasha replies, which is enough for Lemmy to push her angrily against a wall. At which point, their mutual incomprehension plainly acknowledged, silence falls between them. Literal silence, as Godard empties the soundtrack of dialogue, music and ambient sound until we hear Lemmy's voice-off saying, in the laconic tones of hard-boiled narration, 'It's always the same. One never understands anything. And then, one evening, you end up dying of it.' The use of the voice-off gradually assumes greater significance, as we will see.

The most powerful weapon in Lemmy's armoury of light is given to him by Henry Dickson, the other secret agent from the Outerlands, as he expires in a shabby hotel room (see Appendix, 1 Sequence 3). It is a book of surrealist poetry, Paul Eluard's *Capitale de la douleur*. Armed with this 'codebook', Lemmy becomes the agent of lyric illumination, the guardian of all the forbidden words – 'love', 'consciousness', 'tenderness' – which the citizens of Alphaville are daily losing from their lexicon and having whittled from their souls. These ideas converge in a central 15-minute sequence when Lemmy and Natasha are reunited in his hotel room and which marks another crucial stage in Natasha's journey towards the light. The light motifs introduced so far in the film – the electronic light of Alphaville, the light of love and of lyric illumination – are concentrated and developed throughout this sequence.

Having been interrogated by Alpha 60 and shown around its nerve centre, where he learns of the computer's diabolical plans to wage war throughout the galaxy, Lemmy returns to his hotel (see Appendix 1, Sequence 6). In the corridor he sees a man embracing one of the hotel's *séductrices* and notices the sinister detail of a number tattooed on her neck. Making his way to his room, Lemmy is escorted down the corridor by an unfamiliar, raven-haired *séductrice* who sashays alongside him, swinging a set of keys. From the moment in the corridor when the *séductrice* asks Lemmy the forbidden question 'Why?' (prompting an electronic squeal of admonishment from Alpha 60) to Lemmy's later outburst of hilarity at the punchline to 'Story 842', via the rhapsodic lyricism of Lemmy and Natasha's 'love scene', the next 15 minutes will play like a series of musical variations on three words and three questions: 'Why?', 'Where?' and 'What?' *Why?* The question the *séductrice* asks is the same as the one that Natasha comes out with unawares, and when Lemmy points this out she wants to know when she asked 'Why?' (forbidden words are beginning to fall unbidden from her mouth). *Where?* Lemmy subjects Natasha to a kind of softly-softly interrogation routine, in which he wants to discover if she recognises any of the 'secret messages' contained in *Capitale de la douleur*. The aim is for her to reveal that she was born somewhere other than Alphaville. Lemmy prompts her by naming possible places – Florence, Tokyorama, Nueva York – and only the latter brings forth from Natasha an unprompted poetical description – 'Where Broadway sparkles under the snow as soft and gentle as mink' – confirming it as her true birthplace (the language of lyric illumination restores Natasha's memories to her). *What?* The question that Natasha asks of Lemmy and herself – 'What is love?' – follows from Lemmy asking her where she was born, and it finds its answer in their 'love scene'. Bracketed between the moments when Natasha sees a police car pulling up outside the hotel and when the police break into the hotel room, this scene appears to take place simultaneously inside and outside time, with Natasha's poetic recital ending with the room at night. It is as though a whole new day and night have passed and Natasha and Lemmy have together created love's time, which can exist, vulnerable but autonomous, according to its own law beyond Alphaville's time. Robin Wood, too, has commented on this feature of the scene, which he describes as 'the core of the film [...] yet it also covers a long passage of time (just before the police break in, Lemmy is washing, as if to begin a new day)'.[16] It's also worth noting that this sequence does not feature in Godard's treatment, which is otherwise fairly faithful to the action of the finished film, where the description of the action jumps from Lemmy's discovery of the number tattooed on Natasha's neck to the police bursting into the hotel room.

Lemmy and Natasha: love in the light of lyric poetry

The love scene, with its ultra-stylised play of lights, the ritualised movement and postures of Constantine and Karina, and the deployment of Karina's voice, is part dance, part poetry recital. In an essay that explores three 'lyrical interludes' in *À Bout de souffle*, *Bande à part* and *Alphaville*, Adrian Martin has described how 'the lyrical transport provided by a poetic recital does not merely mirror the characters but directly transforms them: from a halting, uncomprehending delivery earlier in the scene, Natasha now magically moves to being a smooth, communicating vessel for verse'.[17] Up to this point in the film, it has only been Lemmy's noirish asides and Alpha 60's stentorian musings that have been granted the status of voices-off on the soundtrack. Natasha's lyrical language distinguishes her words from Alpha 60s distress signals just as it sets them apart from the narratorial characteristics of both Lemmy's and Alpha 60's voice-off. Her accession to this space on the soundtrack signals that the 'light of love' experienced through her eyes now meets the light of lyric illumination expressed through her words. The promise of the coming together in Natasha of eye and voice, sight and speech, image and word endows the sequence with great emotional force, and her recital abounds with clusters of images referring to the motifs of light, circles and lines, as well as suggesting completion and fullness. Her lyrical soliloquy is as follows:

Your voice, your eyes, your hands, your lips.
Our silences, our words.
Light that goes, light that returns.
A single smile between us.
In quest of knowledge, I watched night create day, while we seem unchanged.
O beloved of all, beloved of one alone.
Your mouth silently promised to be happy.
Away, away says Hate. Closer, closer, says Love.
A caress leads us from our infancy.
Increasingly, I see the human form as a lovers' dialogue.
The heart has but one mouth.
Everything by chance.
All words without thought. Sentiments adrift. Men roam the city.
A glance, a word. Because I love you, everything moves.
We must advance to live.
Aim straight ahead towards those you love. I went towards you. I went endlessly towards the light.
If you smile, it enfolds me all the better.
The rays of your arms pierce the mist.

At the end of the 'love scene' Natasha, filmed from outside, stands at the window of the hotel room, her figure visible but almost obscured by the reflections on the glass, a mournful expression on her face and the copy of *Capitale de la douleur* clutched to her chest. She is not yet fully free of Alpha 60; she has the codebook but not yet the full command of the language that might allow her to speak out loud. Among the film's many motifs of light, the window she stands at is a surrealist-tinged surface: half eye, half mirror. For, as Martin Jay has pointed out,

> Many surrealist painters would [...] play on the theme of the window as a transitional or liminal plane between reality and the imagination, foreground and background, external and inner worlds. Often deploying it to suggest yearning for the beyond, they also used the window as an aperture through which a face could look into the shadowy room of the unconscious.[18]

But how do we get from the surrealists to Lemmy Caution? In Godard's hands, Lemmy Caution is a pop art Prometheus whose dialogue could sit comfortably in a Roy-Lichtenstein-style bubble above his head. Pulp haiku – 'Never forget that Revenger and Reporter begin with the same letter' (or, as the subtitles on a recent British print of the film have it, 'Never forget that Journalist and Justice begin with the same letter') – mingle with philosophical *aperçus* lifted straight from Blaise Pascal – 'The silence of those infinite spaces appalled me' – and Henri Bergson – 'I follow the immediate promptings of my conscience'. When Lemmy seeks out his fellow intergalactic secret agent, Henry Dickson, in a seedy flophouse and asks after their colleagues Dick Tracy and Guy L'Éclair (the French name for Flash Gordon), the effect is overwhelmingly collage-like. The film is a tapestry of visual and literary, plastic and semantic references, calling on and culling from pop art and surrealism, film noir and German expressionism, philosophy and pulp novels, *bandes dessineés* and mythology.

The character of Lemmy Caution was created by the British writer (strike-breaker and Fascist organiser) Peter Cheyney. Making his first appearance in Cheyney's 1936 novel *This Man is Dangerous*, Caution would feature in a further ten novels. In 1945 the French publishing house Gallimard inaugurated a new imprint, which enjoyed immediate success in printing French translations of hard-boiled American crime fiction. 'Série noire', the name of the imprint, would become a generic term for a certain kind of pulp fiction, and it is a 'Série noire' edition of Raymond Chandler's *The Big*

Sleep (*Le grand sommeil*) that Lemmy reads, gun in hand, lying in his hotel room. The idea for the 'Série noire' collection was conceived by Marcel Duhamel who had translated works by Dashiell Hammett and Raymond Chandler in the 1930s as well as writing the preface for the seminal study by Raymond Borde and Étienne Chaumeton *Panorama du film noir américain*, which, while not being the first use of the term 'film noir', was the first book about it.[19] Duhamel had also assisted in the development of the surrealist's 'exquisite corpse' game in 1925 as well as participating in the 'researches into sexuality' the surrealists undertook between 1928 and 1932. The first titles published by 'Série noire' were two novels by Peter Cheyney featuring Lemmy Caution: *Cet homme est dangereux* and *La môme vert-de-gris* (*Poison Ivy*, published in English in 1937). It might be going too far to declare that, in *Alphaville*, Godard reclaims Lemmy Caution for surrealism, but these facts certainly put the tough guy's relationship to the poetry of Paul Eluard in a different light. Duhamel's fondness for pulp fiction was no exception among the surrealists, as the American scholar James Naremore has pointed out, quoting the words of the surrealist poet Louis Aragon, who, in 1918, wrote that American crime films

> speak of daily life and manage to raise to a dramatic level a banknote on which our attention is riveted, a table with a revolver on it, a bottle that on occasion becomes a weapon, a handkerchief that reveals a crime, a typewriter that's the horizon of a desk.[20]

Adds Naremore: 'Aragon might well have been describing thrillers of the 1940s, which were perversely erotic, confined largely to interiors, photographed in a deep-focus style that seemed to reveal the secret life of things…'[21] *The secret life of things*: a convertible that's an interplanetary craft, a volume of poetry that doubles as a codebook, a cigarette lighter that's a Promethean torch, not to mention the '$3 Phillips fan, lit from beneath' that often represents Alpha 60 when the computer 'speaks'.[22] In revitalising the film noir connection with surrealism, Godard rediscovers not only the 'secret life of things' but explores the latent possibilities in a standard Lemmy Caution story to reveal what Paul Hammond has described as 'the crux of surrealism … [t]he marvellous – the contamination of reality by the imaginary'.[23]

And then there's Paul Eluard. Detailed studies of Godard's use of Eluard's poetry in *Alphaville* have been carried out by Adrian Martin and Julien

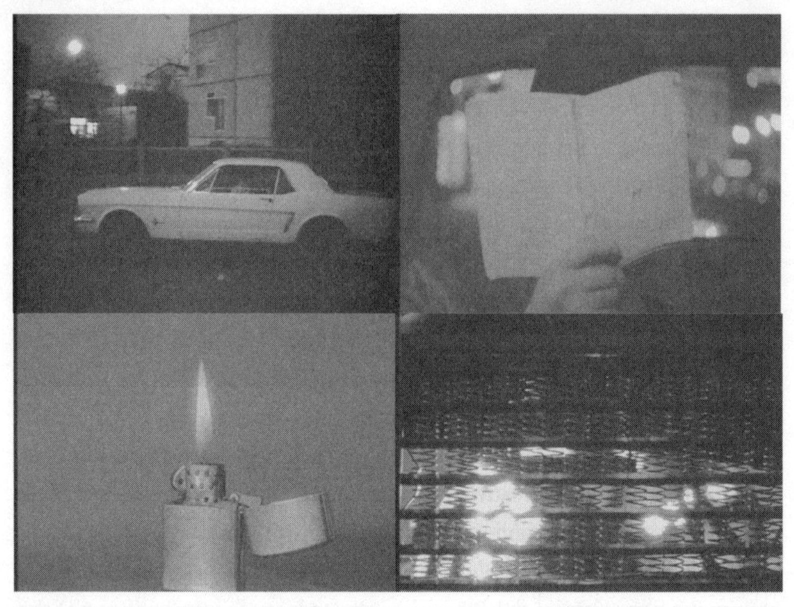

'The secret life of things': Ford convertible as spaceship; *Capitale de la douleur* as codebook; cigarette lighter as Promethean torch; $3 fan as supercomputer

d'Abrigeon, and Martin goes as far as to suggest that not just *Capitale de la douleur*, but 'Eluard's complete poetic oeuvre is the true "underwriting" of Alphaville, in an extensive and fully worked-out way that I believe is singular in Godard's career'.[24] Published in 1926, *Capitale de la douleur* is associated with Eluard's period as a fully-fledged member of the surrealist movement but Godard samples from his later work as well, particularly from *Le Phénix* (1950), with lines from poems in that collection appearing in Natasha's lyrical soliloquy. In fact, as Martin demonstrates, drawing on d'Abrigeon's work, Natasha's speech is 'a gigantic collage of several verses from Eluard taken from different poems'.[25] But Eluard's is a name that carries various associations for Godard; with surrealism and popular love poetry, with the French Resistance and political radicalism. All that surrealism stood for – the creative power of love, the irrational as a liberating force, the 'marvellous' discovered in the everyday – is irreducibly hostile to a technocratic society dedicated to the values of 'logic', 'order' and 'prudence'.

...Light that returns

While *Alphaville*'s surrealist credentials require a certain amount of detective work to uncover, other allusions are more immediately present. Throughout the film Godard makes repeated references to German expressionism and film noir, and nowhere more visibly than in the film's use of black and white, in the deep shadows and blinding lights of its harsh *chiaroscuro*. It's worthwhile hesitating over the terms 'German expressionism' and 'film noir' in order not only to investigate them but also to acknowledge that, in the 40 years since *Alphaville* was made, each has become intimately associated with the other. It's also worth recalling how, even as an established filmmaker, Godard still considered himself a critic. In an interview with *Cahiers* in 1962 he stated: 'As a critic I already considered myself a filmmaker. Today I still consider myself a critic and, in a sense, more so than ever. But instead of writing, I make a film.'[26] If *Alphaville* can be seen as one of Godard's exercises in mimetic film criticism – that is, criticism conducted in the language of the medium – its object is, of course, cinema, and the light that is bought to bear on it is a light from cinema's past, from German expressionism and film noir.

Film noir casts a long shadow. Marc Vernet has situated its origins in the decade 1945–1955, when 'the Americans made it and then the French invented it'.[27] Since then, noir has produced numerous variegations: neo-noir, colour-noir, future-noir, tech-noir. But, in most accounts, film noir is itself infused with the shadows of an earlier cinematic moment when a certain high stylisation – of lighting, acting and set design – preceded and overlapped with a terrible social reality: the fall of the Weimar Republic and the rise to power of Hitler and the Nazis. Few critics can bring themselves to use the term 'German expressionism' without an accompanying flurry of annihilating qualifications. Jacques Aumont, for example, is blunt in his appraisal: 'Expressionism in cinema, German or otherwise, does not exist and has not existed.'[28] For Thomas Elsaesser, contemplating the terms 'German expressionism' and 'Weimar cinema' 'each names an entity that is retrospectively given coherence, because seen from a particular vantage point that compellingly serves a deep-seated need'.[29] Examining the links between expressionism and noir, Vernet observes that

> [i]t has been less frequently noted that the notion of Expressionism itself, in the German domain alone, has served to prove everything and its

> opposite, and that the fashion for it is more a matter of the 1960s, following the appearance of Lotte Eisner's *The Haunted Screen*, than it is of the 1920s.[30]

Vernet disputes the argument that expressionism was 'part of the baggage brought along' by émigrés from Germany and Austria who left Europe before the Nazis took power, but admits that the term has a qualified validity when applied to elements of the image in American cinema of the 1940s and 1950s: the strong oppositions between black and white, the disproportionate shadows accompanying characters, the use of oblique compositions and 'impossible' camera angles. On the role of this lighting style, Vernet emphasises the importance of the light source as not only being visible but being 'exhibited' and 'diegeticized', and offers the following observation:

> In a seemingly paradoxical way, there is a constant attempt to diegeticize this light as a function of the situation (night) and of the light sources (streetlights, lamps), although the light is also exhibited, since the spectator's attention is drawn by its violence, its apparent rarity and the deformations it provokes. But this exhibition is diegeticized in its turn, since the light can be what pursues and threatens the character (it is a persecutory force).[31]

Or, put another way, the light is not only part of the *set* (as a visible light-source – a street lamp, for example) but also part of the *scene* (dictating how much can and cannot be seen) and part of the *story* (contributing to its psychological ambience as a 'persecutory force'). Point for point in his description, Vernet could well be describing *Alphaville*.

But what are we to make of Vernet's suggestion that 'German expressionism' was somehow a creation of the 1960s? The two canonical works of film criticism that are partly responsible for having generated the huge amount of revisionist film history around the term are Lotte Eisner's *The Haunted Screen: The Influence of Max Reinhardt and Expressionism* and Siegfried Kracauer's *From Caligari to Hitler: A Psychological History of the German Film*. Kracauer's study, published in English in 1947, was not translated into French until 1973. However, Eisner's work was translated into French as *L'Écran démoniaque: influence de Max Reinhardt et de l'expressionisme* in 1952, and in a second edition in 1964. Eisner also published a biography of Murnau in 1964, and, throughout the 1950s, was contributing essays on German film to *Cahiers du cinéma* as well as working alongside Henri Langlois at the Cinémathèque Française.[32] Aumont offers the following speculation:

> One day a historian will, no doubt, explain better than I can why it was that the Sixties should have rediscovered and, to my mind, largely invented 'Expressionist cinema'. But it's not overly risky to recall that this discovery, or this invention, took place between the first publication of *L'Écran démoniaque* and the circulation in French art cinemas of the film programme of the same name, that's to say, largely, between 1950 and 1965.[33]

So, *Alphaville* appears towards the end of a period when the 'rediscovery' of German silent cinema, under the influential aegis of Eisner, saw it become 'German expressionism'. Equally fascinating to consider is that the 'invention' of German expressionism ran parallel with the 'invention' of film noir, with the publication in 1955 of Raymond Borde and Etienne Chaumeton's *Panorama du film noir américain*. The connections between the two, now considered so conventional, had yet to be made seriously. In *Alphaville*, Godard the critic-filmmaker makes the connection, as Jonathan Rosenbaum has noted:

> Quite aside from the specific homages (figures clinging to the wall like Cesare sleepwalking in *Caligari*, a track through the hotel's revolving door from *The Last Laugh*, 'Professor Nosferatu', etc.), *Alphaville* has more to say about the silent German cinema than any of the passing references in Godard's essays … it brings social and aesthetic insight equally into focus, and certainly deserves a place next to Kracauer and Eisner.[34]

Rosenbaum observes how the film is constructed around values of light that associate the German silent cinema with the American cinema of the 1940s and 1950s (which was, after all, the cinema that Godard and his colleagues on *Cahiers* had eulogised and analysed before they became filmmakers):

> In *Alphaville*, this shadow is blackness – specifically, the blackness of the German expressionist cinema (*Caligari* and *Lulu*, *Mabuse* and *Metropolis*, *The Golem* and *Faust*) and the cinema that derives from it (*Scarface* and *Kiss Me Deadly*, *Orphée* and *The Trial*). Perhaps the two latter films, in addition to furnishing the Orpheus myth and Akim Tamiroff, also suggested the use of real locations instead of sets. But by relating this use to science fiction (which itself has important links with German expressionism), Godard criticizes the conventions of the genre – and subsequently alters its possibilities, to judge from offspring like *THX 1138*.[35]

But the introduction of the science fiction genre into the film also serves a purpose other than that noted by Rosenbaum. Certainly, it allows Godard to dramatise his theme of the 'presence of the future', but it also allows for a way of revisiting and revitalising elements of the 'fantastic' and 'uncanny' characteristic of German silent cinema, just as in surrealism the revelation of the 'marvellous' in everyday reality was of paramount concern.

Having posed Alpha 60 the riddle that, once solved, will set in train the computer's self-destruction, Lemmy makes his escape, intent on hunting down the professor, only to witness Natasha being taken prisoner (see Appendix 1, Sequence 7). Outside Alpha 60's nerve centre, with the city on the verge of meltdown, he commandeers a car – when the film suddenly and unexpectedly switches into negative, the tonal values of its monochrome momentarily reversed, black becoming white and white black. It's a moment that has flummoxed more than a few commentators. Among them Robin Wood, who has expressed impatience with the sheer excessiveness of these admittedly startling intrusions at the surface level of the film:

> The brief and apparently random excursions into negative perhaps provide distanciation at what might have been mistaken for an exciting climax (or do they intensify the strangeness, hence the terror? – another insoluble ambiguity) and, being illogical, represent a nose-thumbing at Alphavillian logic; but again, these justifications seem too facile to justify so obtrusive an effect, leaving one to conclude that the device itself is facile and that Godard has confused distanciation with distraction.[36]

Wood wasn't able to find a thematic justification for Godard's use of this 'device', either as a riposte to 'logic' or an expression of 'terror', but perhaps that was because he was looking for justification in the wrong places. Writing in *Cahiers du cinéma* in July 1965, Jean-Louis Comolli (who also appears in the film, alongside his fellow *Cahiers* contributor Jean-André Fieschi, as one of the comical duo of scientists Professors Heckel and Jeckell) takes the thematic approach to task. Comolli first proposes how such an approach might account for the sequence printed in negative by relating it to the film's theme and subject and to its place in the film as a whole. In Comolli's somewhat caricatured version of a 'thematic' reading, Lemmy has set Alpha 60 on the path to self-destruction, which the filmmaker justifiably translates 'through an optical effect analogous to a nuclear explosion'. 'I'd like to believe it,' Comolli admits regretfully, 'maybe it's so. But, beside the crudeness and naivety of the explanation, it's redundant.' Whatever the reasons for this mysterious switch to negative, he asserts, it's simpler and more necessary to recognise that it both 'belongs to and responds to the interplay, throughout the film, of light' and that interplay – from harshly

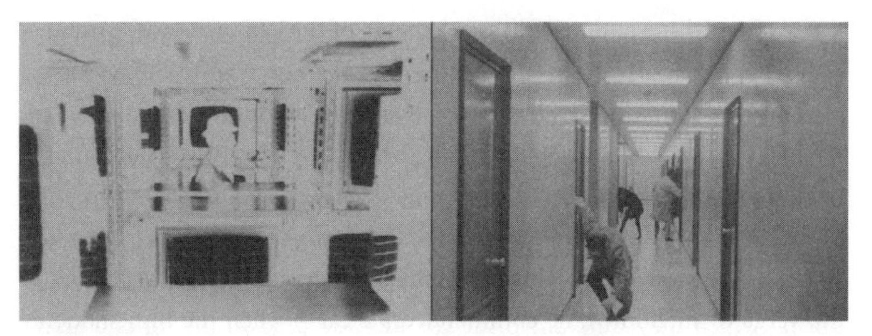

Expressionist quotations: negative printed sequences and corridor caligarisme.

flashing bulbs to subtle variations of natural and artificial light – is part of 'a process of elementary inversion, like the movement of a pendulum between "positive" and "negative" poles'.[37] Where Wood looks for thematic coherence, Comolli establishes a system of plastic values that accommodates the switch to negative rather than treating it as an obtrusive device. Curiously, neither critic examines this moment for what it is, a quotation. Not from one film, but two. In Murnau's *Nosferatu* (1922) and Cocteau's *Orphée* (1949), a negative-printed sequence signifies an uncanny transition from one state of being to another. In both films it is the sign of a passage from the land of the living to the land of the dead. In *Alphaville* (and here the systematic 'equivalence' of plastic values that Comolli identifies in the film, the way in which 'light' can become 'dark' and 'positive' turn to 'negative' as a matter of course, assists a thematic interpretation), Godard reverses the connotation of negative printing as employed in *Nosferatu* and *Orphée* (using the 'negative' of the negative, as it were) to create a sign of transition from the land of the dead (Alphaville) to the land of the living (the Outerlands and beyond).

The circle and the line

At the start of *Alphaville*, Godard displays his medium – light – and his materials – the simple forms of the circle and line. As Alpha 60 introduces us to the story, the two shapes are shown, successively, as a disc of white light and a neon arrow. Having been introduced as graphic elements – that is to say, detached from any specific setting and dominating the screen as illuminated items against a dark background – the shapes are developed throughout the film. When Lemmy arrives at his hotel, the combination of camera movement and setting puts the circle and line to work as components of the *mise en scène*: the camera's semicircular passage through the hotel's revolving doors is followed by its linear ascent in the lift and a backwards tracking shot along the corridor ahead of Lemmy and the *séductrice*, all filmed in a virtuoso single-take. Later, after having met for the first time, Lemmy and Natasha leave his hotel room. In the sequence that follows, during which they walk down the corridor, descend in the lift and arrive in the lobby, the shapes of the circle and line are picked up in further details (see Appendix 1, Sequence 2). Natasha's coat combines both, in its circular hem of white fur that rises into a line reaching halfway up its dark front. The detail of the circle is also carried over into her movements in the lobby, as she turns through 360 degrees on her way to the reception desk to pick up her car keys. Later still, during the scenes in the Institute of General Semantics, the camera's circular movements are linked to both the architecture and the dialogue (see Appendix 1, Sequence 4). As the lights come up in the lecture room and Alpha 60 intones: 'Time is a circle which is endlessly revolving. The descending arc is the past and the rising arc is the future,' the camera describes a circular pan. After the lecture, Natasha descends

The shape of things: circles and lines, staircases and corridors

a spiral staircase and finds Lemmy waiting for her. He tells her that he walked out of the lecture because he couldn't understand a word of what Alpha 60 was saying, and Natasha explains: 'Tonight we learned that life and death exist in the same sphere', and, as she speaks, the camera circles around her. The motif of circularity is accentuated by the linear structure of the pillar against which she leans. From such examples it is evident that the circle and line are integrated into almost every aspect of the film's *mise en scène*, as graphic details (flashing discs, neon arrows), in architectural features (corridors and staircases), as elements of costume design (Natasha's coat) and in camera movement and dialogue.

Given this emphasis, surely these shapes must have specific associations and particular meanings? The first set of meanings could be said to derive from the association of these shapes with character and action – in other words, from their narrative function. Richard Roud has suggested that, for Godard, 'the circle represents evil'.

> So everything in Alphaville that represents the tyranny of the computers is circular. Lemmy's hotel suite is built in circular form; the staircases in the government buildings are spiral; even the city itself is, like Paris, circular, and to get from one place to another one must take a circular route. The corridors may be straight, but one always ends up where one started. And, of course, the computers move in circles. Time, says Alpha 60, is an endless circle. Lemmy, however, maintains that all one has to do is to go straight ahead towards everything one loves, straight ahead: when one arrives at the goal, one realises that one has nevertheless come full circle.[38]

Similarly, Kaja Silverman sees the circle as 'the ubiquitous symbol' of Alphaville and that 'the endlessly repeated "I'm very well, thank you, you're welcome" could be said to circle back upon itself'. Harun Farocki adds: 'Alpha 60 uses the image of the circle to metaphorize the endless present tense of Alphaville.'[39] The circle is thus variously associated with 'evil', 'the tyranny of the computer' and the permanent technocratic 'present tense'. The line is the circle's 'redemptive' opposite, the way forward for the outcasts of Alphaville. All these associations derive from the film's sounds and images, but, while they are extrapolated from the evidence of the film, do they fully explain what the circle and the line 'mean'? To answer this question it is worth considering a second aspect of the film's form, the way in which these shapes contribute to organising the space of the film – in other words, their plastic function.

It is in the architecture of Alphaville, particularly in its corridors and staircases, that the circle and the line find their dominant expression and this directs us back to German silent cinema. In *The Haunted Screen*, Eisner writes about 'the dread' that expressionist cinema associates with corridors and staircases and how, as well as having sexualised connotations, they provide ideal places for the play of light and dark known as *chiaroscuro*. She also comments that what 'the Germans call space [*Raum*] is a concept based half in reality and half in metaphysics';

> [T]he stage and backstage area [*Bühnenraum*] that theatre critics talk about can signify both the limited space visible to the spectator as it can the idea of an unlimited space created onstage by the poet and the extension of the imagination.[40]

Eisner's insight in her description of what she calls *Bühnenraum* directs our attention to the idea of off-screen space. We have already seen how Godard creates a strangely elastic sense of space in the way that he films Lemmy's hotel room. By showing only half of it and leaving the rest more or less to our imagination (or by distorting it, by shooting the reflection of scenes in the bathroom mirror), the circular shape of the hotel room incorporates an off-screen space that is pregnant with possibilities. And, while the circle and the line go towards organising the visible space of *Alphaville*, they are shown to be present at so many levels that they combine to suggest another, potentially infinite, off-screen space. Annette Michelson identifies this formal strategy as a form of cinematic 'dislocation'.

> The city's peripheral avenues, *les boulevards extérieurs*, shift and expand into an irrevocably disquieting suggestion of the routes of interplanetary space. Function and scale of object and place are continuously altered, as image and sound converge upon site and situation in the exploration of the cinematic figure of dislocation.[41]

In a highly detailed 'plastic approach' to *Alphaville*, Bertrand Roussel sees such formal 'dislocation' at work in the film's treatment of perspective. The shot showing Lemmy searching for Natasha in the corridors of Alpha 60 by pushing open door after door is described by Roussel as 'recuperating the perspectival view which has been abandoned to the film's curved motifs [...] as if perspective, rather than being natural, serves as a dramatic element through being successively invoked and abandoned'.[42] Or, put another way, Lemmy is simply going in a 'straight line towards what he loves'. But that 'straight line' is created by a combination of framing, architectural detail and camera movement, elements of the film's form that are set against its wider repertoire of curved, circular and spiral forms. Beyond these interpretations of them, the circle and line are also basic geometrical shapes. Which brings us to science.

$E=mc^2$

'One line of mathematical symbols can contain a whole universe,' observes Ivan Tolstoy. Albert Einstein's formula contains our universe, in which the energy (E) of an object is equivalent to its mass (m) multiplied by the square of the speed of light (c^2).[43] First published in 1905, Einstein's formula for the special theory of relativity was demonstrated to devastating effect 40 years later on 6 August 1945, when an atomic bomb was detonated over the Japanese city of Hiroshima. *Alphaville* is made in the light of this terrifying moment of Promethean self-consciousness. It is a film of its time, in which the atomic brinkmanship of the Cold War threatened to ignite the apocalypse, particularly during the Soviet–American stand-off of the Cuban Missile Crisis in October 1962, and it joins a roster of films dealing with the fear of planetary destruction, including *Kiss Me Deadly* (Robert Aldrich, 1955), *On the Beach* (Stanley Kramer, 1959), *The World, the Flesh and the Devil* (Ranald MacDougall, 1959), *Hiroshima mon amour* (Alain Resnais, 1959), *La Jetée* (Chris Marker, 1962) and *Dr Strangelove, or, How I Learned to Stop Worrying and Love the Bomb* (Stanley Kubrick, 1964). $E=mc^2$ is given a couple of decorative cameos in the film as a kind of neon logo, although it could well be the city's heraldic symbol (with atom rampant), and is set alongside another apocryphal formula, $HF=MC^2$.[44] Einstein's isn't the only illustrious name from 20th-century physics invoked by Godard; the city has a 'rue Enrico Fermi' and a 'boulevard Heisenberg' as well as a 'Mathematics Park'.[45] But are these merely in-jokes which only the *cognescenti* can congratulate themselves on understanding? I'd say not. Godard goes further than name-checking famous physicists, just as he goes beyond simply dramatising atomic fear. He uses the resources of cinema to represent scientific ideas. Consider the choice of a neon light sculpture to represent $E=mc^2$, for example. On the one hand, it's a work of art, as Einstein's formula has often been described. On the other, it's made in a medium that depends on the atoms of a gas (neon) being apparently transformed into energy when ionised by an electrical field, which causes electrons to flow through the gas and light to be emitted. We may recognise the formula without knowing what it means but the neon logo shows us what it means. However, Godard's ambitions extend beyond this simple demonstration. One might say that he made *Alphaville* with a Peter Cheyney novel in one hand and a book about atomic physics in the other, using cinema as a tool of scientific knowledge at the same time as delivering the latest adventures of Lemmy Caution.

Surprisingly few commentators have examined Godard's fascination with scientific theories and his attempt to incarnate them in cinema. One who has is Jean Douchet. In an essay entitled 'Le théorème de Godard', he claims that the director is 'seeking to adapt cinema to today's scientific knowledge'. Douchet continues:

> The other arts – music, painting, architecture – have long done so. Cinema, for the time being, is still stuck with the narrative style of the nineteenth century and can't get shot of it. Godard knows that this position is no longer tenable and that this form of narrative must be utterly modified. So he abides by the knowledge of contemporary science and applies it. So we find in his films the theory of relativity, quantum physics, the uncertainty principle, chance and discontinuity.[46]

Not a bad haul of subjects for a 20th-century filmmaker. But in which films do we find them treated, and how do they appear? Douchet briefly mentions later films such as *Passion* (1982), *Détective* (1984) and *King Lear* (1987), and observes that what animates Godard's interest in science is the idea of 'energy':

> As the basis of the universe, [energy] becomes Godard's fundamental subject, at least in his later films. [...] In the context of his materialist way of thinking, what is bought to the fore is the role and importance of light. This was already starting to appear in *Passion*, whose subject is light. But in previous films and, in particular, in *Alphaville* its role is already important. It is the first film where Godard directly addresses this subject, the relationship of light and energy.[47]

How does this manifest itself? 'Materially, that's to say visually, onscreen', says Douchet, 'as energy working through light.' It is through this 'play of light and energy' that Godard obliges us to re-think what we know and to integrate what scientific knowledge tells us into our lived experience, given that it's already there like a kind of social schizophrenia between the fact of our constantly making use of all the entitlements of modern science while absolutely refusing to integrate what this implies for our own ways of living, thinking and feeling.[48]

Douchet's assessment might appear extreme. Godard's followers are relatively well accustomed to him assuming the roles of 'essayist', 'painter', 'pedagogue' and 'historian' and being treated with respectful seriousness by his numerous exegetes. But 'Godard the scientist'? More like the nutty professor. There are good reasons, though, for Godard to consider cinema as a legitimate tool of scientific knowledge. After all, from the beginning of the 20th century, cinema introduces time to the art of the image just as Einstein, with the theory of relativity, proposes space and time as being inseparable, as they are in cinema. And, if the time of *Alphaville* is tricky, multidimensional (the future seen in the present via the light of the past), then how could its space be otherwise? Lemmy makes a couple of gnomic pronouncements that should alert us to the central role that geometry plays in the film's treatment of scientific themes. After having left the Institute of General Semantics with Natasha, Lemmy goes into voice-over narration, saying, with uncharacteristic geometrical precision, 'We took the tangent to the edge of the circle to the central precincts' (see Appendix 1, Sequence 4). Later, during his first interrogation by Alpha 60, the computer asks him a series of test questions, during which one of their exchanges goes as follows (see Appendix 1, Sequence 5):

Alpha 60: You have come from the Outerlands. What did you feel as you passed through Galactic Space?
Lemmy: The silence of infinite space appalled me.[49]

Lemmy's reply is a quote from the philosopher and mathematician Blaise Pascal (1623–1662), and the spectacle of the hard-boiled private eye laconically mouthing the words of the 17th-century sage must have struck many viewers as either hilarious or pretentious, or both. Why Pascal? Remembered mostly now for his *Pensées*, a posthumously published collection of essays that define a particular Catholic conception of God's grace and from which Pascal's 'wager' derives, in his lifetime Pascal was recognised as a mathematical and scientific prodigy, and it is towards two of his youthful achievements that Godard gestures. In his late teens Pascal invented a machine

The neon world: formula and globe

known as the 'Pascaline', acknowledged to have been (in design if not manufacture) the first digital calculator, which he developed to help his father's work as a tax collector. In quoting Pascal to Alpha 60, Lemmy is already playing a game with the machine, reminding the super-advanced offspring of its humble origins in 17th-century mathematics and tax collecting. As a young man, Pascal also made significant advances in the field of geometry, producing several essays on the subject and developing important theorems in what is known as 'projective geometry'. Which brings us back to the circle and the line. As a film 'about light', *Alphaville* is inevitably a film about optics and, hence, about geometry.

In *Alphaville*, the circle and the line are what links the real world of Paris, 1965, to its transformation into the cinematic image of Alphaville. As basic geometrical shapes, they are part of the process that Michelson calls 'dislocation' and that Roussel explores relative to the film's manipulation of perspective. For it is not just that *Alphaville* creates the future from the present, hence constructing Alphaville from Paris. Rather, the film is a demonstration that such a transformation is inherently *cinematic*, that, even in revealing the presence of the future, the cinematic process transforms, distorts, 'dislocates' a three-dimensional space into a two-dimensional representation. There are sound geometrical reasons for this. What we call 'perspective' is the name given to a process of mapping a three-dimensional space into a two-dimensional representation and is based on geometry ('geometry' means 'measurement of space'). The photographic image, and by extension the cinematic image (which introduces time into the two-dimensional representation of three-dimensional space), transforms conventional Euclidean notions of space:

'From an empirical standpoint, the space of the land surveyor, the architect, the mechanical engineer, that is, the space of practical life, may be regarded as Euclidean space.'[50] But what about the filmmaker, who takes his images from the 'space of practical life' and then reanimates them in cinematic space? What do we call his space? We call it 'non-Euclidean', based on the principles of 'projective geometry'. For nearly 2,000 years after they were proposed in *Elements of Geometry* (300 BC), Euclid's five postulates were the basis for what is known as 'elementary' (or Euclidean) geometry.[51] In the 17th century an architect from Lyons, Girard Desargues (1593–1662), of whom Pascal was a disciple, had the revolutionary idea that a set of parallel lines can be regarded as passing through a point at infinity which 'seems to us to be a natural development of perspective, the visual cone and the vanishing line'. But it took Johannes Kepler, a century later, followed by a former engineer in the French army, Poncelet, to revive Desargues.[52] From the moment they first appear on the screen – as graphic images removed from any perspectival depth – to their absorption into almost every element of the film's form, the circle and the line act as emblems of Godard's emphasis of the transformative nature of cinematic space. A corridor comprises two parallel lines meeting at the vanishing point, a spiral staircase is a cone, and each participates in creating an illusion of depth. Then, an image suddenly appears – a flashing arrow, a neon formula – in which the lack of 'depth' reminds us of that illusion. But, while the effect of this shuttling back and forth between depth and lack of depth in the image may well have the effect of reminding viewers that what they are watching is 'only a movie', that's not all it does. The revolution in space and time that was proposed by the general theory of relativity meant that the claim that a unique geometry could be known to hold true of the world a priori no longer appeared viable. In parallel with this, cinema proposed its own 'distortion' of Euclidean space by adding time to the tradition of perspective inherited from painting and photography. Hence Godard's insistent play on geometry – as light and line, idea and form – to refer to and represent the ideas underpinning the new world of Alphaville.

Alphaville is not just an anti-technocratic squib (though it is that) nor is it simply a Romantic lament at science's unweaving of nature's wonders (though it is that, too). It is, first and foremost, a work of *cinema* – that is, artistic expression in a machine medium dependent on the laws of optics.

Moreover, *Alphaville* demonstrates that Godard was fully conscious of the paradox of using such a medium to express scepticism of technology by the way in which he incorporates the paradox, internalising it and making it part of the film's form. As a film 'about light', *Alphaville* is necessarily a film about the way in which optical laws obtain in cinema and which acknowledges that for cinema to show the world is to distort and dislocate it. Godard attempts to combine poetry and science in the film, to integrate the 'light' of the Romantics with the 'light' of the atomic age. European Romanticism of the 19th century defined itself in part through its vociferous scepticism towards science and the idea of technological progress, the canonical expression of which took shape around Sir Isaac Newton's experiments in optics during the 18th century. Newton investigated the properties of white light using glass prisms, demonstrating that light was wavelike rather than particulate in nature. His dissection of the phenomenon of the rainbow into light of different wavelengths would lead on to Maxwell's theory of electromagnetism and Einstein's special theory of relativity. Keats famously responded to the publication of Newton's *Opticks* (1704) with the barbed verses of *Lamia* (1820):

> Do not all charms fly
> At the mere touch of cold philosophy?
> There was an awful rainbow once in heaven:
> We know her woof, her texture, she is given
> In the dull catalogue of common things.
> Philosophy will clip an angel's wings,
> Conquer all mysteries by rule and line,
> Empty the haunted air, and gnomed mine -
> Unweave a rainbow, as it erewhile made
> The tender-person'd Lamia melt into a shade.[53]

The German poet and scholar Johann Wolfgang von Goethe, too, had embarked on what his British biographer describes as 'a forty year long campaign, which can fairly be called obsessive, to establish a non-Newtonian theory of colour' and which culminated in the publication of *Zur Farbenlehre* (*On the Theory of Colour*) in 1810.[54] When Godard is dubbed a 'Romantic' it is a highly self-conscious kind of Romanticism that's being described, in which the relationship between art and science plays a formative role. In *Alphaville* he managed to combine the best of both. After all, in his quest for cinematically poetic forms by which to express scientific ideas and in his condemnation of their technocratic abuse, Godard had both Keats' sanction and Goethe's as well as that of Nils Bohr, the father of quantum mechanics, who said: 'When it comes to atoms, language can only be used as in poetry. The poet, too, is not nearly so concerned with describing facts as with creating images.'[55] From science we turn to technology, and the fear of it that was abroad when Godard was making *Alphaville*.

The robots are already here!

The weekly news magazine *Le Nouvel Observateur* gave over the front cover of its edition of 6 May 1965 to *Alphaville*, with a banner headline declaring: 'Les Robots sont déjà là!' Across a double-page spread, a couple of scientists from the Centre of General Semantics – Professor Kauffman, a mathematician and Dr Jacques Sauvan, a developer of computers and 'thinking' machines – offered their observations on Godard's dystopian fable. Remarking that Alpha 60 was modelled on the recently developed Bull computer Gamma 60, they agreed that the film's idea of a 'schism between the technocrats and the people' was accurate and that this extended into the world of politics. 'What isn't fictitious is that citizens are no longer considered as electors but as consumers,' observed Professor Kauffman:

> Having transformed the voter into a consumer, the technocrat then 'places' a government in power as they would a washing powder in a supermarket, by calculating demand. This transformation is a collective crime the consequences of which cannot be calculated.[56]

Another aspect of the film's vision rang true: the scientists agreed that 'the impoverishment of language and the simplification of syntax are real' and that they considered this as inevitably accompanying the 'robotization' of humanity.[57] In retrospect, what's interesting about their account is how closely the two scientists saw Godard's vision as corresponding to contemporary trends. A certain kind of futurism was clearly very much of the cultural moment, and attitudes towards it oscillated between uncertainty and euphoria, between suspicion of the computer and of technocratic trends generally and enthusiasm for headlong modernisation. In interviews on the film's release, Godard was sceptical about the technocratic tenor of the time. Alphaville is a state that has succeeded in transforming citizens into consumers, where life itself is standardised, 'as in a society of termites or ants'. 'The film takes place at a moment when communism and capitalism aren't political antagonists but simply two different systems of planning,' he explained. 'One seeks to programme the mind before the body, the other works in reverse.'[58] (Godard gives this political observation a comical twist in Lemmy's masquerade as 'Ivan Johnson', reporter for the '*Figaro-Pravda*' newspaper, a name derived from two famous dailies, one French and right-wing, the other Soviet [see Appendix 1, Sequence 1].) Against the mantra of 'planning', he counterposed poetry and romanticism: 'Alphaville is a world without romanticism. The world of the *grands ensembles* is a world that attempts to eliminate adventure in favour of planning. The duty of the artist is to set traps for the planners.'[59]

To set traps for the planners: which is what Lemmy Caution must do in order to short-circuit Alpha 60, to trap the thinking-machine into thinking like a human being in order to solve the puzzle he sets it, at which moment the machine will become, as Lemmy predicts, 'my likeness, my brother' (see Appendix 1, Sequence 5). *Alphaville* inherits a theme that runs throughout the history of cinema: the encounter between man and machine. The potential for drama or comedy in this encounter derives not from the smooth execution of man's plans by the machine but from a scenario that asks: 'What plans do machines have for man?' The dramatic mainstays of the man–machine encounter are automation and malfunction. It's a guarantee of humanity that a man should be able to cause a machine to malfunction, not in the name of some strategic kind of Luddism but as the assertion of human autonomy *by accident*, when the proverbial spanner is thrown in the works (or when a man wielding a spanner is dragged into the works, like Chaplin in *Modern Times*). But when man becomes part of the machine, another cog or circuit or, worse still, a technocrat – that is, one who doesn't simply labour but who has internalised the logic of technology so thoroughly that he simply becomes a reflexive adjunct to his machine, a tool in his own turn, one who doesn't feel alienated from machines but integrated with them – then, clearly, the stakes are even higher.

Throughout the 1960s French modernisation resounded with declarations of 'the new' in which the idea of technocracy played a major role. As a term that had emerged in the United States after the First World War, 'technocracy' described 'rationalised industrial democracy'. The cultural historian Kristin Ross has chronicled the emergence of the term in the post-war 'reordering' of French culture, describing it as being 'especially visible after 1958 when De Gaulle consolidated his return to power surrounded by, for the first time, an elite and overt entourage of *ministre-techniciens*'.[60] The figure of the technocrat was a type characteristic of the times, whether as the *jeune cadre* ('young executive') – 'well shaven and armed with a steadfast faith in a technologically perfected future' – in novels by Simone de Beauvoir and Christiane Rochefort, or as the output-obsessed businessman, who contrasts with the bumbling, old-world figure of Monsieur Hulot in Jacques Tati's films *Les Vacances de M. Hulot/Monsieur Hulot's Holidays* (1953) and *Playtime* (1967).[61] As a recognisable sociological type, known as 'organisation man' in Anglo-Saxon parlance, the technocrat was the new man par excellence of post-war French consumer modernity, a being devoted to the cult of efficiency, in which the system of values was defined by technological rationality. Confident that such values were sufficiently widespread to constitute a veritable ideology, Godard lampoons them in *Alphaville* by presenting a society in which *techné* has overwhelmed *demos*, a computer-controlled society ordered according to the dictats of 'prudence, control and security'. In his caricature of the technocratic image, Godard presents two sorts of technocrat, the functionary and the visionary. The technocratic functionaries in *Alphaville* include the white-coated Chief Engineer (Laszlo Szabo) and Professors Heckell and Jeckell (their names taken from a pair of cartoon characters), who, when not sniggering at Lemmy's old-fashioned camera, call and respond in a mechanistic litany of cause-and-effect statements ('Grand Omega minus will bring victory to …' '…anti matter'). The technocratic visionary comes in the shape of Professor von Braun, the scientist whom Lemmy must either persuade to return with him to the Outerlands, or kill.

If, as Ross asserts, 'technocracy' was one of the terms that was active in the battle around the word 'man' taking place during the era of French modernisation, the other, which proved highly influential at the level of intellectual enquiry, was 'structuralism'.[62] Ross paraphrases the critique of structuralist thought by the philosopher Henri Lefebvre, for whom 'structuralism was nothing more than the infusion of technocratic thought into the intellectual field', as follows:

> The structuralist crisis of 'man' and 'humanism' was above all a practical and historical crisis bought on by a capitalist society where unchecked bureaucratic

growth mean that institutions – medicine, teaching, research – no longer put humans first. [...] But instead of analysing (much less proposing a direction for transforming) that society, structuralism served as an underlying ideology justifying the devaluation of humans under capitalist modernization ... The idea that society was composed of agentless structures helped reinforce people's growing sense that the future was not in their control, or that it would play itself out as a kind of slow petrification, that their life was defined by lifeless, meaningless, and unchanging bureaucratic structures ruled by no one.[63]

Godard had asked Roland Barthes, one of the leading proponents of structuralist literary criticism, to play the role of a scientist in *Alphaville* but Barthes had declined because, according to Godard, he was 'afraid of being made to appear ridiculous'.[64] Barthes' reputation for forensically dissecting the accoutrements of mass culture – from cars to movie stars, fashion to food – as the ahistorical masks of petit bourgeois culture rested on his famous collection of short essays entitled *Mythologies,* originally published in 1957. It is intriguing to speculate on how Barthes might have featured in *Alphaville.* After all, the filmmaker's close attention to consumer culture was as penetrating as the writer's, but there is plenty of evidence to indicate that Godard had a more than ambivalent attitude towards structuralist ideas when it came to film criticism. For one who has the reputation of being 'the film theorist's favourite filmmaker', Godard expressed a surprisingly straightforward hostility towards the structuralist application to cinema of linguistic models of meaning that were being developed by Barthes, Christian Metz and Pier Paolo Pasolini. 'We are the children of the language of cinema. Our parents are Griffith, Hawks, Dreyer, and Bazin and Langlois but not you,' Godard berated the structuralists in an account of the heated exchange that took place between Barthes and the *Cahiers* critic Luc Moullet at the Pesaro Film Festival in 1966. 'Anyway, how can you address structures without sounds and images?'[65] For Marc Cerisuelo, Godard's hostility towards structuralism in its heyday was based on his being 'viscerally attached to existentialism, to Sartre and Merleau-Ponty', and that not to think about cinema in its own terms – that is, as sounds and images – was 'the supreme evil'.[66] In retrospect, Barthes' unwillingness to participate in *Alphaville* appears quite understandable.

'There are several attitudes possible when confronted with a "terroristic" work,' Pierre Samson mused in the left-leaning periodical *Les Temps*

Modernes, slipping off his critical gloves before vigorously setting about Godard, whose work he saw as having been animated by a 'terroristic' spirit ever since *À Bout de souffle*.[67] For Samson and others the best form of defence was attack, and *Alphaville* met with its share of well-aimed brickbats. It's putting it delicately to claim that Godard divided opinion. For some he was a 'genius' and *Alphaville* 'probably [his] masterpiece, one of the three or four most important films made in France since the war'.[68] For others he was a 'sham', whose work betrayed a 'right-wing, petit-bourgeois, romantic' sensibility.[69] Such sharp critical divisions nonetheless contributed to 'the extraordinary success of what one might well name "the Godard phenomenon" which was in full swing by the mid-1960s'.[70] Part of Godard's reputation was based on what the young Bernardo Bertolucci dubbed his 'vulgarity', adding that for him this was a positive quality: 'I call "vulgarity" his capacity and his ability to live day to day, close to things, to live in the world as does a journalist, always aware of the right time to arrive on the scene.'[71] Outside France, others had also noted the unique combination of seemingly scattershot cultural references and of-the-moment social observation that characterised his filmmaking. In her 1968 essay 'Godard' Susan Sontag recognised the 'casually encyclopaedic' nature of his work, and the American critic Richard Roud lauded his sensitivity to emerging cultural currents, most notably in his film *La Chinoise*, the portrait of a group of Maoist students that predated and, for some, anticipated the student uprisings of May 1968.[72] Godard was sensitive to this aspect of his work and commented on the perceived appeal of *Alphaville* at the time of its release: 'I give people the impression of having finally taken on the big questions. *Alphaville* expresses certain current ideas that are, let's say, the flavour of the month.' But he was quick to qualify this perception: '*Alphaville* doesn't deal with issues any more serious or profound than those addressed in *Vivre sa vie* or *Une Femme mariée*. It's just that it's a more general subject than the others.'[73] The cinematic bravura on display in the film's transformation of Paris into Alphaville, the present into the future, was commended by the majority of French reviewers, some of whom recognised that *Alphaville* was as much 'about' the power of the poetic imagination as it was about topical issues that could be gathered under the modish rubric of 'technological alienation'. *L'Humanité* described *Alphaville* as 'adapting modern poetry to the language of cinema' and Gilles Jacob, for whom it was the director's best film to date, perceptively noted that 'the passage from one state to another … appears to be one of Godard's dominant preoccupations'.[74] (Jacob was also one of the very few critics who, beyond commenting on Alpha 60's startling vocalisations, considered the significance of the film's soundtrack, observing how 'highly worked' it is and how much the film's 'impact and effect' depend on it.)[75]

Others were less convinced. Regarding Godard's vision of Paris as a futuristic dystopia, Samson was scathing: 'Godard only chooses the most exterior details, he contents himself with naming things at the expense of knowing how to show them … He inhabits the level of a sort of exoticism of automation and modernism.'[76] Furthermore, Godard's emphasis on the values of love, culture and individual liberty over the dehumanising modern world were, for Samson, shoehorned into the old story of St George saving the fair maiden from the dragon but retold as Lemmy Caution rescuing Natasha von Braun from Alpha 60. The film 'is the very image of the enemy inside us that needs to be beaten,' Samson declared; namely

> the constant temptation to fall back on petit-bourgeois individualism in the face of fear of the unknown and when confronted with having to integrate the new way of life and new aspects of reality into a coherent politics. *Alphaville* is one the most 'demoralising' films around. It would like to show us the impossibility of any revolt, the decline of mankind in a controlled economy and the uselessness of all political systems.[77]

That a film 'quite as manifestly reactionary' as *Alphaville* had managed to 'mystify' the leftist critics of *L'Humanité* and *Le Nouvel Observateur* mystified Samson in turn. Drawing no consolation from the opinion of the right-wing daily *Le Figaro* (which had proclaimed that 'it takes a lot of nerve to serve up a work which contains quite such a mixture of good and bad, and to deliver in so serious a tone a message so cluttered up with naivety and childishness'), Samson could only put his comrades' lapses down to the fact that, because Godard 'shoots without long preparation, and improvises against a very thin canvas', this permits him to 'stay in the current of fashionable ideas, to be at one with the snobberies and curiosities of the moment'.[78] Other left-leaning critics opted not to put the boot in quite as firmly as Samson but to persuade the filmmaker gently towards the 'scientific' approach of Marxist methodology. The critic for *France Nouvelle* thought that *Alphaville* confirmed Godard as 'one of the most important directors in France' but, like Samson, saw him as identifying only 'the exterior signs of a real malaise', conferring on them 'a sort of metaphysical dimension' and ignoring 'the social forces' working through them.[79] Like many other commentators, the writer picked up on comments Godard had made in his interview with *Le Monde*, where he stated that he did not confuse Soviet Communism with Marxism, which, for him, was 'altogether different, a way of thinking, an ideology'.[80] 'From which one could conclude that ideologies simply float in a state of privileged intellectual abstraction', the writer responded, comparing Godard to other key auteurs of the period, Antonioni, Bergman and Fellini, who, while producing works that were 'not negligible' as indicators of the modern world, could not describe 'the possibilities of the future' because their thinking was not founded on 'all-encompassing scientific observation'. It was, the critic deduced, because of such 'confusion' that Godard had chosen science fiction as a kind of 'refuge' from which to utter 'the cry of an anguished humanist intellectual'.[81]

One of the most representative critiques of Godard's cinema appeared, like Samson's onslaught, in the pages of *Les Temps Modernes*. Less thoroughly hostile than Samson, Bernard Dort unpicked Godard's method of filmmaking in order to uncover its underlying sensibility. Dort summarised Godard's vision of cinema accurately, as being 'simultaneously, a means of recording the world, and an instrument of knowledge and revelation'.

> In fact, even as he pretends to be shooting documentaries which deliver both the reflection and the truth of beings and things, Godard, while claiming for himself absolute objectivity, never stops contrasting the fragility of a present that knows only how to deteriorate with the myth of an ancient order in which beings and things were fully themselves and which is no longer accessible to us except through death or art.[82]

While overwhelmingly negative in tone, this is a pretty good definition of the Romantic sensibility that one can indeed find at work throughout Godard's early phase and, particularly, in *Alphaville*. Although Dort doesn't use the term, preferring to castigate Godard for his 'nostalgia', what he is describing could be called 'alienation', or 'disenchantment'. Godard has frequently expressed his enthusiasm as a youth for the work of early German Romantic luminaries, especially Novalis, and during this phase of his filmmaking 'alienation' was not simply a theme but also a register. A theme, in the sense that modernity, through the growth of science and technology, the division of labour and a competitive market economy, was seen to have 'alienated' people from themselves, each other and nature. And a register, in that art was seen as the primary means of 're-enchanting' the world. 'The aim of the artist,' Novalis wrote, 'is to romanticise the world, to see the infinite in the finite, the extraordinary in the commonplace, the wonderful in the banal.'[83] Which could serve well as a motto for Godard's approach to his material in *Alphaville*, in his transformation of the modern city with its brutalist architecture and technological accessories into a world where, magically, future and past coexist. And, if 'the mission of Romantic art is to restore unity and its purpose was to restore the magic, mystery and beauty of nature that had been lost with the growth of science and technology', then surely the character of Natasha von Braun assumes the dimensions of a fully-fledged Romantic heroine. The last words she speaks on her journey from transcendental homelessness towards the light are: 'I love you' (see Appendix 1, Sequence 7). More than simply providing the film with its distinctly un-Godardian happy ending, they are a declaration of faith in the Romantic *credo*.[84]

In *Alphaville*, the past is not simply the world from which Lemmy Caution arrives, nor is it some nostalgically ideal hinterland, as Dort suggested. The old question of 'What plans do machines have for man?' receives an answer from the past that haunts *Alphaville*. Several critics have noticed that Godard scatters his film with references to Nazi Germany: the numbers tattooed on the skin of the *séductrices*; the telling name change of Natasha's father from Nosferatu to von Braun; and the 'SS' on a lift button, which, shot in such emphatic close-up, clearly doesn't simply signify 'basement' ('sous-sol'). In his review, Georges Sadoul recounted:

> In May 1945, in the hall of a grand Parisian hotel, similar to the one in *Alphaville*, I saw a crowd of deportees crushed together wearing tattooed numbers as, by chance, I was reminded when watching the newsreel that accompanied the screening of the film.[85]

Such details of Nazi barbarism were public knowledge in 1965 and Godard alludes to them not just to induce an arguably tasteless frisson of historical dread. Professor von Braun, the technocrat-dictator, carried a name that was full of recent historical resonance. Wernher von Braun was the name of the Nazi scientist who had been involved in developing the massively destructive V2 rockets towards the end of the Second World War. He had been among a select group of Nazi scientists whom the Allies had spirited out of Europe after the war, in an operation known as 'Paperclip', so that they could contribute their expertise to American research. When the Apollo 11 rocket left its launch pad at Cape Canaveral in July 1969, von Braun was one of several former Nazis proudly observing their handiwork on its journey into space.[86] And how much did Godard know about the 'strategic alliance' between International Business Machines (IBM) and the Nazis in the extermination of the Jews?[87] In the light of such details, Natasha von Braun's own collar of numbers is almost too close to the bone. In 1964 the philosopher Herbert Marcuse, himself an émigré from Nazi Germany, published one of the key texts of social criticism in the 1960s, *One-Dimensional Man*. In its conclusion, he wrote the following:

> Auschwitz continues to haunt, not the memory but the accomplishments of man – the space flights; the rockets and missiles, the labyrinthine basement under the Snack Bar; the pretty electronic plants, clean, hygienic and with flower beds; the poison gas which is not really harmful to people; the secrecy in which we all participate.[88]

Notes

1. Baby, 'Dresser des embuscades dans le planification'.
2. Marker, Chris, 'Marker direct', *Film Comment*, May–June 2003, p. 39.
3. Perez, Gilberto, *The Material Ghost: Films and their Medium* (Johns Hopkins University Press, Baltimore and London, 1998), p. 354.
4. Charles Bitsch, Godard's assistant on *Alphaville*, informs me that the man whose voice was used for Alpha 60 had been operated on for throat cancer and had been trained to speak from his diaphragm, a 'slightly less romantic account' than the standard one, which states that the voice was that of a war veteran whose throat had been shot out in combat.
5. Coutard, Raoul, 'Light of day', *Sight and Sound*, Winter 1965/1966.
6. MacCabe, Colin, *Godard: A Portrait of the Artist at 70* (Bloomsbury, London, 2003), p. 119; Marie, Michel, *À Bout de souffle étude critique* (Nathan, Paris, 1999), pp. 55–56.
7. Interview with Coutard.
8. Interview with Coutard.
9. Douin, Jean-Luc, *Jean-Luc Godard* (Rivages, Paris, 1989), p. 161.
10. Silverman and Farocki, *Speaking about Godard*, p. 60.
11. Ibid. p. 64.
12. At 14 years of age, Karina was due to play Mary in a film about Christ that Dreyer was planning, but he was never able to make it. See Bergala (ed.), *Jean-Luc Godard par Jean-Luc Godard*, vol. 1, p. 37.

13 Aumont, Jacques, *Du Visage au cinéma* (Éditions de l'Étoile/Cahiers du cinéma, Paris, 1992), p.10.
14 Perez, *The Material Ghost,* p. 353.
15 Vincendeau, Ginette, *Stars and Stardom in French Cinema* (Continuum, London and New York, 2000), pp. 115–116.
16 Wood, '*Alphaville*', p. 90.
17 Martin, Adrian, 'Recital: three lyrical interludes in Godard', in M. Temple, J.S. Williams and M. Witt (eds), *Forever Godard* (Black Dog Publishing, London, 2004), p. 263.
18 Jay, Martin, *Downcast Eyes: The Denigration of Vision in Twentieth-Century French Thought* (University of California Press, Berkeley, 1993), p. 245.
19 Borde, Raymond and Chaumeton, Étienne, *Panorama du film noir américain* (Éditions de minuit, Paris, 1955). The term 'film noir' was first used by Nino Frank in 'The crime adventure story: a new kind of detective film', *L'Écran Français* 61, 1946 and J.P. Chartier, in 'The Americans are making dark films, too', *Revue du Cinéma* 2, 1946, both quoted in Barton R. Palmer, *Perspectives on Film Noir* (G.K. Hall and Company, New York, 1996).
20 Naremore, James, *More than Night: Film Noir in its Contexts* (University of California Press, Berkeley and London, 1998), p. 18.
21 Ibid. p. 18.
22 Godard, Jean-Luc, *Introduction à une véritable histoire du cinéma* (Éditions Albatros, Paris, 1980), p. 93.
23 Hammond, Paul, *The Shadow and its Shadow: Surrealist Writings on Cinema* (British Film Institute, London, 1978), p. 19.
24 Martin, 'Recital: three lyrical interludes in Godard', p. 264. See also d'Abrigeon, Julien, *Jean-Luc Godard, cinéaste écrivain: De la Citation à la création, presence et rôle de la littérature dans le cinéma de Jean-Luc Godard de 1959 à 1967*, http://tapin.free.fr/godard/memoire.html#reseaux, 2004 (accessed April 2004).
25 Martin, 'Recital: three lyrical interludes in Godard', p. 264.
26 Bergala (ed.), *Jean-Luc Godard par Jean-Luc Godard,* vol. 1, p. 215.
27 Vernet, Marc, 'Film noir at the edge of doom', in J. Copjec (ed.), *Shades of Noir* (London, Verso, 1993), p. 1.
28 Aumont, *Du Visage au cinéma,* p. 199.
29 Elsaesser, Thomas, 'Expressionist film or Weimar cinema? With Seigfried Kracauer and Lotte Eisner (once more) to the movies', in T. Elsaesser (ed.), *Weimar Cinema and After: Germany's Historical Imaginary* (Routledge, London and New York, 2000), p. 21.
30 Vernet, 'Film noir at the edge of doom', p. 1.
31 Ibid. p. 9.
32 Eisner's *The Haunted Screen* was first published in French as *L'Écran démoniaque: Influence de Max Reinhardt et de l'expressionisme* in 1952 by André Bonne, Paris and then again in 1964 by Le Terrain Vague. Her biography of Murnau, *F.W. Murnau,* was published by Eric Losfeld/Le Terrain Vague, Paris 1964. Kracauer's *From Caligari to Hitler* was published in English in 1947 but was not published in French until 1973 by L'Age d'homme, Lausanne.
33 Aumont, *Du Visage au cinéma,* pp. 204–205.
34 Rosenbaum, Jonathan, 'The Criticism of Jean-Luc Godard', in J. Rosenbaum, *Placing Movies: The Practice of Film Criticism* (University of California Press, Berkeley and London, 1995), p. 21.

35 Ibid. p. 21.
36 Wood, '*Alphaville*', p. 93.
37 Comolli, Jean-Louis, 'À rebours?', *Cahiers du cinéma* 168, July 1965.
38 Roud, Richard, 'Anguish: Alphaville', in J.L. Godard, *Alphaville: A Film by Jean-Luc Godard,* translation of screenplay by P. Whitehead (Faber and Faber, London, 2000), p. 16.
39 Silverman and Farocki, *Speaking about Godard,* p. 69.
40 Eisner, Lotte H., *L'Écran démoniaque: Influence de Max Reinhardt et de l'expressionisme* (Éditions André Bonne, Paris, 1952), p. 67.
41 Michelson, Annette, 'Film and the radical aspiration', in P.A. Sitney (ed.), *Film Culture: An Anthology* (Secker and Warburg, London, 1971), p. 411.
42 Roussel, Bertrand, 'Courbes et subversion esthétique: une approche plastique d'*Alphaville*', *CinémAction* 52, 1989, pp. 72–73.
43 Tolstoy, Ivan, *The Knowledge and the Power: Reflections on the History of Science* (Canongate, Edinburgh, 1990), p. 16. David Bodanis tells us that 'c' in Einstein's formula stands for *celeritas*, the Latin word meaning 'swiftness', also the root of our word 'celebrity' (I shall resist a speculative riff on Eddie Constantine and how long it takes for the light from a fading star to reach us). In Bodanis, D., *$E=mc^2$: A Biography of the World's Most Famous Equation* (Macmillan, London, 2000), p. 37.
44 Roussel offers a convincing interpretation of this 'equation': '$hf=mc^2$ is a play on words which only makes sense if one takes "h" to mean "homme" (man) and "f" as "femme" (woman). The resulting equation is, therefore, "homme-femme = aime c'est deux" (mc^2) (man-woman = to love takes two).' Roussel, 'Courbes et subversion esthétique', pp. 68–69.
45 Enrico Fermi (1901–1954) was awarded the Nobel Prize for Physics in 1938. Fermi co-invented and designed the first man-made nuclear reactor, starting it up in a historic secret experiment at the University of Chicago on 2 December 1942. He was one of the leaders of the team of physicists on the Manhattan Project for the development of nuclear energy and the atomic bomb. Werner Heisenberg (1901–1976) was one of the great physicists of the 20th century. He is perhaps best known as one of the fathers of quantum mechanics, the new physics of the atomic world, and especially for the 'uncertainty principle' in quantum theory. He is also known for his controversial role as a leader of Germany's nuclear fission research during the Second World War. The ambiguities attaching to Heisenberg's role in developing the 'Nazi bomb' remain controversial to this day and have been the subject of several major studies, as well as inspiring Michael Frayn's 1998 play *Copenhagen* about the meeting between Heisenberg and the Danish physicist Nils Bohr. The 2003 edition of the script contains a lengthy postscript and post-postscript, as well as a bibliography and other information useful to the general reader wishing to learn more about this fascinating intersection of science and war with political and personal morality. In Frayn, M., *Copenhagen* (Methuen, London, 2003).
46 Douchet, Jean, 'Le théorème de Godard', *Cahiers du cinéma* 'Spécial Godard: 30 ans depuis', November 1990, pp. 12–13.
47 Ibid. pp. 12–13.
48 Ibid. pp. 12–13.
49 Godard, *Alphaville: A Film by Jean-Luc Godard,* p. 54.
50 Pirenne, M.H., *Optics, Painting and Photography* (Cambridge University Press, London and New York, 1970), p. 51.

51 Pedoe, Daniel, *Geometry and the Liberal Arts* (Penguin, London, 1976), p. 142.
52 Ibid. p. 78.
53 See Abrams, M.H., *The Mirror and the Lamp: Romantic Theory and the Critical Tradition* (Oxford University Press, New York, 1953) and Dawkins, Richard, *Unweaving the Rainbow: Science, Delusion and the Appetite for Wonder* (Allen Lane, London, 1998).
54 Boyle, Nicholas, *Goethe: The Poet and the Age*, vol. 1, *The Poetry of Desire 1749–1790* (Clarendon Press, Oxford, 1991).
55 Tolstoy, *The Knowledge and the Power*, p. 15.
56 Cournot, Michel, 'Les Robots sonts déjà là', *Le Nouvel Observateur*, 6 May 1965, pp. 2–3.
57 Ibid. pp. 2–3.
58 Baby, 'Dresser des embuscades dans le planification'.
59 Ibid.
60 Ross, Kristin, *Fast Cars, Clean Bodies: Decolonization and the Reordering of French Culture* (MIT Press, Cambridge, MA and London, 1995), p. 178.
61 Ibid. p. 166.
62 Ibid. p. 163.
63 Ibid. pp. 176–177.
64 Godard, Jean-Luc, 'Lutter sur deux fronts', *Cahiers du cinéma* 194, 1967, in Bergala (ed.), *Jean-Luc Godard par Jean-Luc Godard*, vol. 1, p. 304.
65 Godard, Jean-Luc, 'Trois mille heures de cinéma', *Cahiers du cinéma* 184, 1966, in Bergala, (ed.), *Jean-Luc Godard par Jean-Luc Godard*, vol. 1, p. 294.
66 Cerisuelo, Marc, 'Godard et la théorie: tu n'as rien vu à Pesaro', *CinémAction* 109, October 2003.
67 Samson, Pierre, 'À propos d'Alphaville: les mécanismes d'une imposture', *Les Temps Modernes* 230, 1965.
68 Chapier, Henry, 'Oui a Robbe-Grillet et non à Antonioni et Godard', *Combat*, 5 July 1965 and Aubriant, Michel, *Paris-presse* in Jacob, Gilles, '*Alphaville*: for or against', *Sight and Sound*, Winter 1965/1966, p. 162.
69 Samson, Pierre, 'À propos d'Alphaville'.
70 Prédal, René, 'Godard et la critique', *Jeune Cinéma* 8, 1965, p. 30.
71 Bertolucci, Bernardo, 'Versus Godard', *Cahiers du cinéma* 186, 1967.
72 Sontag, Susan, 'Godard', in *A Susan Sontag Reader* (Penguin, London, 1987), p. 236 and Roud, Richard, *Godard* (Thames and Hudson, London, 1970).
73 *Paris-presse*, 12 May 1965.
74 'Lemmy aux enfers', *L'Humanité*, 9 May 1965 and Jacob, Gilles, 'Alphaville: un cauchemar non climatisé', p. 117.
75 Jacob, 'Alphaville: un cauchemar non climatisé', p. 117; Isabelle Schlemmer called the film's use of sound 'a great success' in *Jeune Cinéma* 8, 1965, p. 3.
76 Ibid. p. 184.
77 Ibid. p. 187.
78 Pierre Mazars paraphrased in Jacob, '*Alphaville*: for or against', p. 162 and Samson, 'À propos d'*Alphaville*', p. 186.
79 *France Nouvelle*, 12 May 1965.
80 *Le Monde*, 6 May 1965.
81 *France Nouvelle*, 12 May 1965.
82 Dort, Bernard, 'Godard ou le Romantique abusif', *Les Temps Modernes*, December 1965, p. 1119.

83 Novalis was the pseudonym of Friedrich von Hardenburg (1772–1801) in Beiser, Frederick, *Routledge Encyclopedia of Philosophy,* vol. 8 (Routledge, London and New York, 1998), pp. 348–352.

84 The term 'transcendental homelessness' comes from Georg Lukàcs, who uses it in his *Theory of the Novel* as follows: 'German Romanticism, although it did not completely clarify its concept of the novel, drew a close connection between it and the concept of the Romantic; and rightly so, for the novel form is, like no other, an expression of this transcendental homelessness.' In Lukács, Georg, *Theory of the Novel* (Merlin Press, London, 1978), p. 41. See also Beiser, *Routledge Encyclopedia of Philosophy,* vol. 8, pp. 348–352.

85 Sadoul, Georges, 'À l'indicatif présent', *Les Lettres Françaises* 13, 1965, p. 7.

86 Bower, Tom, *The Paperclip Conspiracy: The Battle for the Spoils and Secrets of Nazi Germany* (Michael Joseph, London, 1987).

87 Early computer technology, punchcards and punchcard sorting systems were developed by the German-American Herman Hollerith, enabling the organisation and coordination of the Nazi war effort and the extermination of the Jews. IBM had a near-global monopoly on this technology. See Black, Edwin, *IBM and the Holocaust: The Strategic Alliance between Nazi Germany and America's Most Powerful Corporation* (Time Warner Books, London, 2002).

88 Marcuse, Herbert, *One-Dimensional Man: Studies in the Ideology of Advanced Industrial Society* (Routledge and Kegan Paul, London, 1984), p. 247.

3 *Alphaville*: the afterlife

Alphaville (2002); light sculpture by Belinda Guidi

Alphaville is not yet obsolete. It remains a fashionable cinematic icon of monochrome futurism; *Metropolis* for mods. Google Godard and, apart from the tribute sites, you'll come across a number of other Alphavilles: an eighties German pop group, an online chronicle of 'the dark side of digital utopia' and, of course, a Brazilian construction company.[1] The name has clearly proved too good not to be ripped off. Had he patented it back in the sixties, Godard could probably have bankrolled a few more films with the income, but that would have been out of character for a director whose career has been a consistent assault on the idea of intellectual property. So, on the one hand, *Alphaville* has become enough of a cult film for its world to be evoked by its name alone. On the other hand, it has also inspired artists and filmmakers, who, in response to its plastic beauty and formal innovations, have returned to it as an object of creative fascination.

Almost as soon as it was released, *Alphaville* started spawning hybrid tributes, each of them an element of its afterlife. In a suitably idiosyncratic fashion, the film's screenplay was written after the film had been made, not by Godard but by an English filmmaker named Peter Whitehead. Known for his documentaries about 'Swinging London', *Wholly Communion* (1965) and *Tonite Let's All Make Love in London* (1967), Whitehead, like many young filmmakers of the time, was overwhelmed and inspired by Godard's cinema. 'I'd seen *Alphaville* at the London Film Festival and it just possessed me, it was a total revelation,' Whitehead recalls. 'I didn't know how to come to terms with the experience. I'd seen the *Avant-scène du cinéma* screenplays and I suddenly thought, "Nobody's done this in England."'[2] Whitehead approached the film's British distributor, George Hoellering of the Academy Cinema, who put the idea of a published screenplay to Godard, who, for a fee of £200, agreed to the project. Whitehead takes up the story:

> Godard was in London staying at the Hilton. I'd drawn up a contract and was told that I should go and meet him. For me, this was a high point in my life, to meet my hero! I knew all of his films. I'd seen *Vivre sa vie* 12 times! He was sitting in the foyer, I could see the back of his head, so I came up to him and said 'Monsieur Godard?' and he leapt out of his skin. I introduced myself, saying 'I'm the guy who wants to do the screenplay'. 'Oh yes', he said, 'where's the money?'[3]

Whitehead's book inaugurated a genre of film publishing that continues today: the transcription of a film's action and dialogue into the form of a post-facto screenplay. He explains the creation of the screenplay as follows:

> After the film had been made there was a dialogue list which was needed for subtitles. For *Alphaville*, Godard did what he'd never done before, which was to produce a treatment, which is also in my book. What's interesting is how the finished film *does* relate to the original treatment, but when I came to make my book there was effectively no screenplay. So, for three weeks, I sat at a Steenbeck with a 35mm print of the film going through it frame by frame, scene by scene, describing the action and translating the dialogue.[4]

While it's possible to be retrospectively exact and clarify aspects of Whitehead's screenplay (the translation of 'la conscience', for example, which also means 'consciousness' is rendered throughout as 'conscience'), it's equally important to recognise it as an interpretation of the film as much as a reliable screenplay. Whitehead's book is an example of the aide-mémoire as a therapeutic exercise, a report from an imagination so possessed by a film that it must, in turn, try to possess the object that exercises such power.

Whitehead is by no means alone in having been possessed by *Alphaville*. In March 2000 a series of unusual screenings took place at the BFI IMAX cinema on London's South Bank. *Alphaville* was to be a sonic *objet trouvé* in the hands of Scanner, an electronic sound-artist and musician who made his name by collecting ('scanning') short-wave gobbets of chatter and static and rearranging them into a kind of ambient *musique concrète*. In keeping with his working method, Scanner had chosen to combine samples of the film's French-language dialogue with snatches from the English version, as well as playing fast and loose with Paul Misraki's original score of urgent klaxon-like tones and stabbing strings. In short, Scanner was intending not merely to rescore *Alphaville* but to remix the film's entire soundworld, an approach guaranteed to outrage purists. It was a high-risk strategy open to accusations of glib appropriation and disrespect towards the original film. Such misgivings missed the point of the exercise.[5] In one respect, Scanner's interventionist approach can be said to have been highly respectful towards an aspect of Godard's filmmaking, its intense and striking attention to sound. The soundworld of *Alphaville* – presided over by the harsh and disturbing tones of the computer, Alpha 60, at the same time glotally human and gratingly electronic – provided the alibi for such a treatment. In addition, as a visual corollary to this manipulation of the film's sonic textures, *Alphaville* was to be projected through an anamorphic lens in an IMAX cinema. Not that the film sat comfortably on the vast screen, the 84 by 40 feet dimensions of which put one in mind of Fritz Lang's famous dismissal of the Cinemascope format as fit only for 'filming snakes and funerals'.[6] *Alphaville* was to be doubly distorted: once at the level of its soundtrack and twice through anamorphic projection. (Anamorphic lenses are usually fitted onto 35mm film projectors in order to project films shot in Cinemascope. *Alphaville*, however, was shot in the standard 35mm Academy ratio, and when projected through an anamorphic lens its images came across as excessively stretched, warped and distended.) Was this a way of presenting a film the canonical cult status of which might otherwise

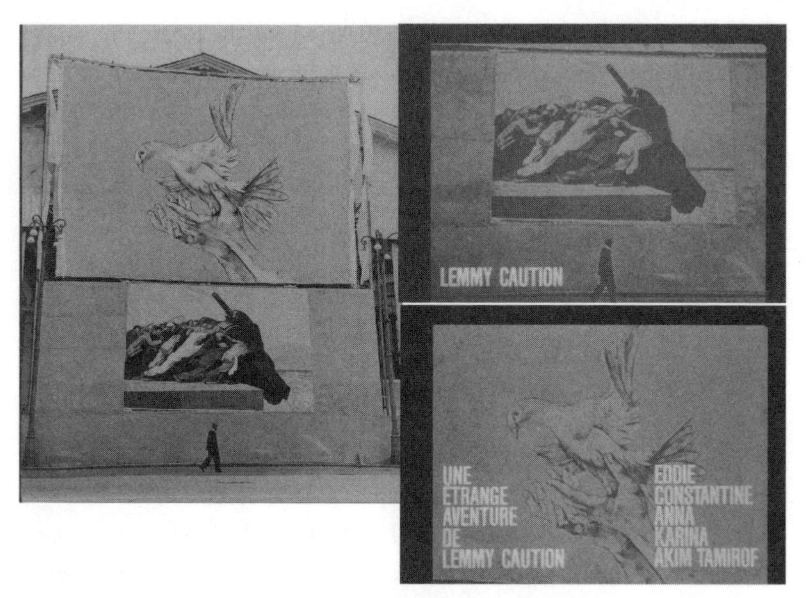

Chris Marker's photograph of a Moscow street scene, as filmed by Godard for the credits sequence of *Alphaville* (photograph courtesy of Chris Marker)

make the experience too comfortable, too familiar? No doubt. This was projection conceived as an act of grand magnification and distortion, and which brought to mind those films that delight in using time-lapse photography to reveal hidden dimensions of time and scale unavailable to the human eye: flowers blooming, glaciers melting, the dawn-to-dusk life cycle of a city. The film that had succeeded in 'making strange' the spectacle of 1960s Paris was itself made strange anew that night.

Later the same year, in Paris, I came across another example of *Alphaville* being re-examined through other methods of distortion and magnification. An exhibition at the Swiss Cultural Centre entitled 'Paris-Godard: la ville, la politique, le langage' used frame enlargements and sound details from *Alphaville* and *Deux ou trois choses que je sais d'elle*, exhibiting them in a form of what might be called 'three-dimensional montage'.[7] Each film had a room to itself in which isolated elements were displayed. The staging of *Deux ou trois choses* emphasised the strong primary colours of its Eastmancolour film-stock, its jaundiced perspective on consumerism and its use of the Techniscope framing to shoot new housing developments in the Paris suburbs. *Alphaville* was presented in small, single images of the city: a ghostly, monochrome future-world where the poetry remained intact. Both the IMAX and Swiss Cultural Centre events were attempting to create what might be called 'immersive' approaches to the film: through an unnatural scale of projection and an overwhelming sound environment in one case, and, in the other, through a kind of architectural reordering, allowing visitors to walk through the films and 'inhabit' them anew.

Two time-travellers: Godard and Marker

Deep within the mnemotechnic labyrinth of Chris Marker's 1997 CD-ROM *Immemory* one comes across an image that features in the credit sequence of *Alphaville.*[8] It is a photograph, taken by Marker, which assumes an enigmatic status in Godard's film. The photograph shows a street scene: a man, frozen in mid-stride, features as a tiny figure at the very bottom of the frame beneath two poster-like images on a wall, the first showing a painted image of a crowd toppling a tank into the sea, the one above, looming larger still, a painting of a pair of hands releasing the dove of peace. Marker took the photograph in Moscow, describing it as 'typical Cold War propaganda'. 'I relate it to my days in the USSR,' he explains, 'which means later than 1957, thus pre-USSR/USA thaw, so probably no later than 1960.' He had no idea that Godard had used it until he saw it on-screen.[9] In Godard's treatment, each of the two poster images within the photograph is reframed. First, the image of the crowd and tank dominates the screen, with the small figure of the static stroller still at the base of the frame and alongside whom the name 'Lemmy Caution' appears in bright white letters before the rest of the titles appear in reverse, and, as they do, the camera pans up to reframe the image of the hands and the dove. Over 30 years later, Marker reclaimed the photograph as one of his own images in his CD-ROM's theatre of memory. Just as Godard incorporated the photograph into the credit sequence of his film, Marker reincorporates the credit sequence into his treatment of the image. The poster of the crowd and tank becomes a (cinema) screen within the (computer) screen on which Marker replays the credit sequence of *Alphaville,* and a strange effect occurs in which the entirety of Marker's photograph is absorbed into one of its details. In *Immemory*, Marker adds a speculative text commentary:

> The people of the world join hands to throw the tanks into the drink (not all of them, as the Czechs and Hungarians will find out later) – there the symbol is clear enough, but whose hands are releasing the dove of peace? A woman's hands, perhaps an angel's. 'Who if I cried out …' Was Godard thinking of Rilke when he slipped this image into the credits screen of *Alphaville*?[10]

'We are before a collage with many levels of meaning and sensation,' observes Raymond Bellour, 'to which is added a reference to the first *Duino Elegy* and to the famous verses cited several times by Godard: "Beauty is nothing – but the first touch of terror."'[11] One could go further in excavating these levels, but a couple are worth emphasising. One of these attaches to the reference to Rainer Maria Rilke, who in 1923, the same year as the *Duino Elegies*, published his *Sonnets to Orpheus*, and the figure of the mythical poet has a resonance in *Alphaville* and more widely in Godard's work that I will consider later. The other is more obvious but no less multifaceted and has to do with the possible relationships between Godard's and Marker's work, more specifically between *Alphaville* and *La Jetée* (1962).

While there isn't space here fully to explore the affinities between the two filmmakers, it's worth sketching some of their shared history. Both are associated with the new wave, although Marker started making films in the early 1950s. While Godard cut his teeth as one of the polemical, ground-breaking critics on *Cahiers du cinéma*, Marker, who was also a writer and photographer in the 1950s, was affiliated with a loose grouping of filmmakers that became known as the 'Left Bank' group and included Alain Resnais and Agnès Varda. In 1967 Godard contributed to the portmanteau film *Loin de Vietnam* (*Far from Vietnam*), an expression of anti-Vietnam War solidarity, which Marker was involved in coordinating and editing with the group SLON (Société pour le Lancement d'Oeuvres Nouvelles).[12] Beyond a background in the new wave and an involvement in radical political filmmaking from the late 1960s, it is through their innovations in film form that Godard and Marker have remained allied. Unlike Godard, Marker has never made 'conventional' cinema, if, by that, one means feature-length fiction films. He has concentrated instead on what might loosely be called the 'documentary essay', of which he is generally acknowledged to be the principal living exponent, and his work extends across many media including television, gallery installations and CD-ROM. And while Godard has remained obdurately resistant regarding the possibilities of the so-called 'digital revolution' he was working with video in the early 1970s, producing his own essays for French television as well as incorporating video in his feature films, and, throughout the 1980s and 1990s, labouring on the eight-part video *magnum opus* of *Histoire(s) du cinéma*. What justifies setting *La Jetée* and *Alphaville* side by side, apart from the fact that they make the ideal new wave sci-fi double bill?[13] Perhaps it's best to start with what sets them apart. *La Jetée* is a *photo-roman* ('photo-novel') of 28 minutes and its form is what most distinguishes it from Godard's film. Composed almost entirely of black and white still images, *La Jetée* tells the story of a soldier who, in the ruins of post-apocalypse Paris, is used as a guinea pig in time-travel experiments. He guards in his memory an 'image of childhood' so strong that it allows him to travel back through time and, eventually, into the future, where it is hoped he will discover the means to save the human race. The image that proves so powerful is that of a man dying on the main pier of Orly airport. Rather than opt to travel into the future, the time traveller chooses to flee to the past to be reunited with a woman he has fallen in love with. His captors send an assassin after him, who, one morning on the pier of Orly airport, kills him. The image that the soldier has guarded and that has allowed him access to every dimension of time was that of his own death. Widely regarded as being not only one of the greatest of science fiction films but also a work of true originality, *La Jetée* is a meditation on the cinema as a time machine. It is famous for the moment when a woman's eyes open from sleep at 24 frames per second, a moment arrived at through a refined, rhythmic panoply of cross-fades, superimpositions and fades to black. Her opening eyes become the film's emblem of time; movement animates the stills and cinema is awoken from a *photo-roman*. What the two films have in common, other than being war-haunted works inhabiting a historical context full of dread, is how they find their 'special effects' in the most fundamental of cinematic resources: time is both the subject and substance of *La Jetée*, just as light is in *Alphaville*.

Science fiction films tell us as much about the time in which they were made as the future they project, and between the two moments – the one specific, the other nominal (1984, 2001, etc.) – a sense develops of their qualities of prescience and allegorical vision. The enterprise of proposing a world-to-be is always a hostage to the future's fortune. The law of diminishing returns that applies with regards to special effects bears this out. How soon before *Matrix*-era 'bullet time' looks as dated as Douglas Trumbull's 'star gate' pyrotechnics in *2001: A Space Odyssey* (Stanley Kubrick, 1968)?[14] Which may explain why *Alphaville* hasn't aged as badly as other examples of the genre; it finds its 'special effect' in the specifically cinematic resource of light. But this light, let's remind ourselves, is the light of the past brought to bear on the presence of the future *now*. Would it be going too far to suggest that, in adding the dimensions of past and future to the present of 1965, Godard was able to set the controls of his particular time machine to withstand the very test of time? There's no shortage of films that seek to travel in time following *Alphaville*, from *Blade Runner* (Ridley Scott, 1982) and *Mauvais sang* (Leos Carax, 1986) to *Gattaca* (Andrew Niccol, 1997) and *Dark City* (Alex Proyas, 1998). There is also the developing genre of what critic Jonathan Romney has named 'steel and glass cinema', which he describes 'as cinema set in the recognisably contemporary urban world but framed and shot in such a way that it becomes detached, not unreal so much as irreal, bordering on science fiction', examples of which include *Elle est des nôtres* (*She's a Jolly Good Fellow*, Seigrid Alnoy, 2002), *DemonLover* (Olivier Assayas, 2002), *Cypher* (Vincenzo Natali, 2002) and *Code 46* (Michael Winterbottom, 2003).[15] Romney claims *Alphaville* to be 'the mother' of such cinema, and with good reason. In the 40 or so years separating *Alphaville* from *DemonLover* it has become evident that the no-place of Godard's dystopia, with its labyrinth of corridors and lobbies, was already one big non-place in waiting. The presence of the future that Godard was keen to capture back in 1965 has since taken shape as a global non-place crossing continents and time zones. 'It may be that we have already dreamed our dream of the future,' J.G. Ballard has mused, 'and have woken with a start into a world of motorways, shopping malls and airport concourses which lie around us like a first instalment of a future that has forgotten to materialize.'[16] Or, to put it another way, Alphaville exists. Everywhere.

Lemmy *redux*

> And so the final battle commences, the battle between money and blood.
>
> Lemmy Caution, *Allemagne année 90 neuf zéro* (1991)

In 1991, 26 years after making *Alphaville*, Godard released a sequel to the film entitled *Allemagne année 90 neuf zéro*. Although it was advertised as such – the publicity for the film's American release announced 'from the creator of *Alphaville*, the further adventures of Lemmy Caution' – *Allemagne année 90* can hardly be considered to be a sequel in any conventional sense. Yet there are more than merely echoes and correspondences between the two films; in *Allemagne année 90* Godard makes explicit references to *Alphaville*, and these allow for a comparison to be made between the styles of Godard's 'early' and 'late' work. Eddie Constantine assumed his Lemmy Caution persona for the last time in *Allemagne année 90*, playing the grizzled, shabby 'last spy' of the former Communist state of East Germany. Rendered redundant by the 'end of history' and coming in from the Cold War, Lemmy makes his way across zones of dereliction towards Berlin and the West. Exuding an air of world-weary decrepitude, the 'revenger-reporter' of *Alphaville* cuts a figure full of pathos. Already employed by Godard in the 1960s to portray a man from the past, in *Allemagne année 90* he appears positively prehistoric. What *Allemagne année 90* has in common with *Alphaville* is Godard's desire to set past and future in the present tense, albeit without the generic alibi of science fiction. Just as the future was already becoming visible in the architecture and technology of 1960s Paris so there is, in *Allemagne année 90*, the desire to depict the German state at a moment of historical transformation, between the fall of the Berlin Wall in 1989 and national reunification on 3 October 1990. Elegiac and melancholic in tone, *Allemagne année 90* is representative of what one critic has called the 'doomed European vein' of Godard's later work, in which the director offers 'one of the most dense and intensive of [his] recent films, an aesthetic and philosophical meditation on the solitary "state" of post-Communist East Germany'.[17]

Allemagne année 90 was commissioned in 1989 by the French television channel Antenne 2, which had asked Godard to make a film about 'the state of solitude' and received in return a film about 'the solitude of a state'. Somewhat less than feature length at 62 minutes, the film is nevertheless as densely allusive a patchwork-palimpsest as any of Godard's later works.[18] What remains of *Alphaville* in *Allemagne année 90*? In the first part of the film, 'Variation 1: le dernier espion' ('First variation: the last spy'), certain motifs seem to be reprised in the shots of illuminated arrows and circular lights. Lemmy's cursory debriefing with Count Zelten (Hans Zischler) of the Deuxième Bureau in the shabby back room of a hairdressing salon irresistibly recalls a similar encounter a quarter of a century earlier between Lemmy and Henry Dickson in the Red Star Hotel, but this time with Constantine in the role of the elderly and disoriented spy played in *Alphaville* by Akim Tamiroff. And, just as *Alphaville* is haunted by the past, *Allemagne année 90*, too, has a cast of ghosts. As Lemmy crosses the river to West Berlin we hear him intone a line from *Nosferatu*: 'As I crossed the frontier, the phantoms came to meet me.' In Murnau's film, these are the words of Hutter (the Jonathan Harker figure in the film, played by Gustav von Wangenheim) as he approaches the fiend's castle and enters the land of the undead; in Godard's, the line is reprised with mordant irony – the 'phantom' Lemmy sees is a jogger. But whereas in *Alphaville* the references to the haunted black and white of German expressionism illuminate an association of ideas – the lighting of Nazi rallies linked to Karl Freund's lighting of expressionist films, technocratic efficiency associated with National Socialist tyranny – the ghosts at large in *Allemagne année 90* have generally been summoned from further back in Germany's past. At every stage of his journey towards the West, historical figures arrive from a parallel dimension of time to meet Lemmy, often in the form of citations and quotations from music, painting and literature (and, of course, cinema), and sometimes as characters, such as the woman who tells him that she has been both Dora, the patient of Freud, as well as Charlotte Kersner, Goethe's lover and a character in the author's *The Sorrows of Young Werther*. In 'Variation 2: Charlotte à Weimar' ('Second Variation: Charlotte in Weimar'), Dora-Charlotte conveys Lemmy through time back to Weimar as remembered by Goethe, Schiller, Kafka and Liszt. But by far the most direct reference to Alphaville comes in the closing scene of *Allemagne année 90*, which ends where *Alphaville* begins, with Lemmy Caution in a hotel room in a strange city. Whereas in *Alphaville* Lemmy was pitted against Alpha 60, man against machine, in *Allemagne année 90* he observes 'a desperate struggle under way in the cities of the world where money has come to reign supreme'. The reference to the earlier film becomes more explicitly developed as the scene goes on. Just as it did in *Alphaville*, Lemmy's bedside table holds the ubiquitous Bible, and the aged spy has only to open it for the memories to come flooding back – memories he greets with a despairing exclamation of 'Oh, the bastards!' ('O, les salauds!').[19] And just as Lemmy encountered Natasha von Braun in his hotel room in *Alphaville* so, in *Allemagne année 90*, he discovers the young woman who, in the East, used to work for him as his maid, on her knees, making up his bed. Their exchange is brief and bitterly ironic:

Lemmy: So, you've chosen liberty too?
Maid: Arbeit macht frei!

Godard shoots this exchange from Lemmy's perspective as he stands over the young woman and she replies to his question with a quotation: 'Work makes you free', the words that emblazoned the entrance to Auschwitz. And swelling on the soundtrack, as if moaning through the hotel room itself, is a howling wind. The wind from the East, perhaps?[20] Or the sound of the storm rising in an angel's wings? Another ghost that haunts Godard's work is the great German critic Walter Benjamin, who interpreted the figure of an angel in a painting by Paul Klee, *Angelus Novus*, as 'the angel of history'. Benjamin wrote, 'His face is turned towards the past.'

> Where we perceive a chain of events, he sees one single catastrophe which keeps piling wreckage upon wreckage and hurls it in front of his feet. The angel would like to stay and make whole what has been smashed. But a storm is blowing from Paradise; it has got caught in his wings with such violence that the angel can no longer close them. The storm irresistibly propels him into the future to which his back is turned, while the pile of debris before him grows skyward. This storm is what we call progress.[21]

The references to *Alphaville* allow the viewer a way into *Allemagne année 90*, but only so far. There's no denying that Godard's later work, while often of a rich and sensual beauty, is characterised by a dense and frequently hermetic network of references. In his review of *Éloge de l'amour* (2001), Jonathan Rosenbaum starts by citing Manny Farber's admission of 34 years earlier: 'No other filmmaker has so consistently made me feel like a stupid ass.' 'Today Godard is just as intimidating,' Rosenbaum adds. *Plus ça change*... He goes on to list some of the cinematic references recognised in *Éloge* – among them *Pickpocket* (Robert Bresson, 1959), *L'Atalante* (Jean Vigo, 1934) and *The Apple* (*Sib*, Samira Makmalbaf, 1998), as well as nods to Roberto Rossellini and John Ford.[22] Also writing about *Éloge*, Adrian Martin has expressed similar sentiments but in tones of greater frustration:

> Godard sometimes makes the viewers feel [...] like ashamed ignoramuses: didn't you know that the train station sign 'Drancy-Avenir' is also the title of

> a recent political film? Can't you recognize all those Parisian sites where the key moments of the French Resistance played themselves out? Didn't you appreciate the profundity of the citation from Bresson?[23]

From the days of the new wave to now, an expression of critical befuddlement has been one of the standard responses to Godard's work; the critics scratch their heads and admit: 'I didn't get all of it, but…' Anything else would be less than honest. There's a scene in *Allemagne année 90* that has attracted the attention of several commentators in this respect. Towards the end of the film, in 'Variation 6: le déclin de l'Occident' ('Sixth Variation: the decline of the West'), Lemmy finally makes it to the West. Before arriving at his hotel, he haunts the night-time streets and gazes at the illuminated windows of a car showroom. We see the image of a couple, frozen like mannequins, sitting in a bright red car. Over this shot Lemmy talks about a young couple named Hans and Sophie Scholl who were arrested and killed for distributing anti-Nazi tracts during the Second World War. A shot of a white rose appears on-screen and the sound of a typewriter is heard. These three elements – Lemmy's narration, the image of the white rose, the sound of a typewriter – have, as Godard admits, 'no relationship for the spectator. But a relationship exists.'[24] What is the relationship? On the one hand, it is between an image, a sound and a historical fact: the resistance group that Hans and Sophie Scholl founded at the University of Munich in June 1943 was called the White Rose Movement, under which name they distributed typewritten calls for resistance to the Nazis. But this fact is concealed beneath the image and sound even as it is alluded to in the unusual force of their combination. As Lucie Dugas has pointed out, this places the spectator in a paradoxical position:

> On one hand, Godard asks that the spectator has the necessary knowledge to get what he's saying but, on the other hand, he wishes this to remain submerged by the image and sound and only to bear fruit through what they reveal, which is hardly possible if one doesn't understand the references he calls on.[25]

As spectators we are, as Dugas notes, in 'a labyrinth' of signs. We sense that this combination of image and sound, of rose and typewriter, has an allusive force, but we do not know to what it alludes. One of the reasons for this has to do with the proximity of *Allemagne année 90* to *Histoire(s) du cinéma*, the series of videos on which Godard was working, on and off, between 1989 and 1998. Some 265 minutes long and divided into eight episodes, *Histoire(s)* is an illustrated commentary on a lifetime's work, criticism in the form of a video essay in which Godard refines his ideas about cinema and its characteristics, its achievements and failures. *Histoire(s)* is an immensely ambitious work of collage comprising excerpts from films and photographs, details from painting and written texts, interviews and musical citations, in a labyrinthine video-palimpsest that can be seen to have influenced other works made by Godard during the same period.[26] *Allemagne année 90* was one such work, and, while the 'White Rose' sequence is indicative of the style of videographic montage that characterises *Histoire(s)*, there are many other such moments in *Allemagne année 90*. What both works reveal is how, while he remains the same inveterate collagist he was in his early films, Godard's approach to form has developed new dimensions. Images now surge forward and reveal themselves from beneath others, then sink away again, their arrangement no longer being only 'horizontal' (one following another) but 'vertical' (one concealing another). Hence my use of the term 'palimpsest', which, while referring to a much-written-over text, goes some way towards indicating the extraordinarily multi-layered nature of Godard's arrangement of image and sound. In the days of *Alphaville* Godard's quotations, while not exclusively drawn from cinema, were sufficiently within the realm of *cinéphile* competence to be relatively accessible. Since *Histoire(s)* the range of references has become so bewilderingly wide, as well as recondite, that they intimidate as much as the form of their arrangement dazzles. Clearly, we need someone to guide us through this labyrinth into the light.

Orpheus unbound

> I regret not knowing how to sing, otherwise I think I'd sing a lot.
>
> Jean-Luc Godard, April 2001

In *Alphaville*, Orpheus, Bard of Thrace, the poet and singer of classical myth, undergoes one of his most unlikely reincarnations as Lemmy Caution rescuing Natasha von Braun, his Eurydice. As they flee together he tells her, with inverted fidelity to the myth, not to look back at the underworld they've escaped from.[27] Godard's version of the myth draws heavily on its earlier cinematic treatment in Jean Cocteau's *Orphée* (1949). When he filmed *Orphée*,

Cocteau was adapting his play of 1926 as well as updating the myth by dressing it with all the trappings of modern life. Cocteau's Orphée (Jean Marais) hangs out at the Café des Poètes, is conveyed to the land of the dead in a chauffeured limousine (which passes through a negative-printed landscape) and receives communications from the dead poet Cégeste (Edouard Dermite) via the car's radio. In *Orphée*, radio and cinema are technologies transfigured, machines that communicate mediumistically with those who know how to listen and see, those with the capacity to tune into the other-worldly wavelengths on which myth broadcasts its messages from beyond. The strange communications that Orphée picks up are a kind of morse code in blank verse – 'L'oiseau chante avec ses doigts. Une fois. Je repète. L'oiseau chante avec ses doigts. Deux fois. Je repète…' ('The bird sings with its fingers. Once. I repeat. The bird sings with its fingers. Twice. I repeat…') – and they echo throughout *Alphaville*, either as aphoristic fragments from the mouth of a machine in the questions that Alpha 60 poses Lemmy, or when Lemmy narrates, in voice-off, his taxi ride with Natasha after they have left the Institute of General Semantics (see Appendix 1, Sequence 4):

> Lemmy (off): As the radio was issuing its traffic programme, Natasha spoke to me in her voice of a pretty sphinx…

The words 'joli sphinx' ('pretty sphinx'), thrice repeated on the soundtrack, work with the mention of the car's radio to reprise the mysterious communications in *Orphée*. There are also numerous visual invocations of Cocteau's film, from the negative-printed sequences already discussed to the scenes in which inhabitants stagger through the corridors of Alphaville as the city self-destructs, clinging to the walls like the deathly denizens of *Orphée*'s 'Zone' (see Appendix 1, Sequence 7). Paul Eluard, too, finds a place in Godard's Orphic myth as the figure of the dead poet whose words are bought to life by his messenger-surrogate Lemmy Caution. All of which indicates that, for Godard, the myth of Orpheus serves a greater purpose than merely *homage*. In 1962 Godard was already calling on Cocteau's film as providing a definition of cinema as 'the only art which, to use Cocteau's phrase, "films death at work". The person one films is in the process of ageing and dying, so one films a moment of death at work.'[28] Over 30 years later, in episode 2A of *Histoire(s) du cinéma*, *Seul le cinéma*, the reference has changed slightly (Cocteau's name has gone missing) but the aim is still to give a definition of cinema in terms deriving from myth and poetry: 'Cinema authorises Orpheus to turn round without causing Eurydice's death.' For Godard, cinema not only shows but also conquers death.

Myths, as we know, never die; they just assume new disguises. Claude Levi-Strauss observed that the interpretations of myths 'are themselves instances of the myth, prolongations or variations of its narrative logic'.[29] So it is with Orpheus, who has been busy reinventing himself since he last plucked his lyre. In a brilliant essay that anatomises the place of this myth in Godard's work, Jacques Aumont claims that the director has often returned to *Orphée*, and, in *Alphaville*, *Allemagne année 90* and *Hélas pour moi* (1993), he finds the film's 'disguised remakes'.[30] Orpheus is the 'code name' for cinema, which possesses 'the power to look behind itself and, in the same look, to bring history forward and to make it disappear'.[31]

> Filmed, the past freezes, but can die no longer. [...] Such is the horizon of the Orphic metaphor: the cinema is that which endows us with another memory...Cinema remembers everything, virtually and sometimes for real, but it has changed our way of remembering ourselves, changed the contents of our memory, changed memory itself.[32]

In Cocteau's film, Orphée is guided through the Zone, wading in slow motion through the limbo between the lands of the living and the dead; 'time is the wind he must walk against'.[33] Could it be the same wind invading Lemmy's hotel room at the end of *Allemagne année 90*? If so, this wind makes twins of Orpheus and Benjamin's Angel, both of them travelling in time, continually turning back to look at where they've come from, caught at the moment of crossing a boundary, one passing from the darkness of the underworld to the light, the other propelled forward from Paradise by 'progress'. As Aumont acknowledges, the Orphic metaphor for cinema at work in Godard's films is ambiguous. In having looked back at the past, cinema casts its light forward in time as well: cinema 'projects'.

Alphaville is just such a projection, a vision of the city of the future as a *Lichtdom*, a 'cathedral of light', bought to the screen in the haunted shadow of German expressionism.[34] What haunts expressionism? On the one hand, it is haunted by association with the moment in German history when mass spectacle met blood-and-soil barbarism in the aestheticisation of politics that Walter Benjamin saw as a tell-tale sign of fascism. But, on the other hand, expressionism is haunted, in its 'foretelling' of fascism, by a kind of clairvoyance. *Light that goes, light that returns*: projected once in German silent cinema, projected twice in Nazi spectacle. Godard's invocation of such light in *Alphaville* signals his subscription to the idea that cinema is both historical echo chamber and early warning system, an idea fully developed in *Histoire(s) du cinéma*. When, in Episode 2B, *Fatale beauté*, he tells us that 'Murnau and Freund invented the lighting of Nuremberg when Hitler didn't even have beer money in the Munich bars' he is condensing, in a pithy aphorism, an idea that is already at work in *Alphaville*, in its haunted light of the past projected into the present-future of Paris 1965.[35] Godard's originality lies less in the idea itself than in the way he applies it. Others, such as Siegfried Kracauer and Georg Lukács, were attributing nascent fascist tendencies to expressionist aesthetics in the 1930s. What Godard claims is that it is cinema's unique capacity to have represented in embryo what was to come:

> Cinema communicates in advance great shifts that are going to occur. And it's in this sense that is shows illnesses before they become visible. It's an external sign that shows things. It's a bit abnormal. It's something that's going to happen, like an irruption.[36]

Cinema communicates in advance. The *Oxford English Dictionary* tells us that 'Orphic' also means 'oracular'. In his recent study of oracles, *The Road to Delphi*, Michael Wood opens by asking a question: 'What do we make of the extended metaphorical afterlife of oracles?' He answers with references ranging from classical myth to contemporary fiction, from a visit to the doctor to the reading of newspaper horoscopes, from stock market forecasts to the vogue, after-11 September 2001, for the prophecies of Nostradamus. The concept of the oracle finds us automatically keeping company with charlatans and mysteries, credulous humans and 'intelligent' machines, all busy consulting runes, seeing portents, finding the future in the past. As Wood observes:

> It is a subtle suggestion that the future, undetermined until particular individuals or societies move toward it, but determined in all kinds of ways once they do, always hides in the past, and in theory could always be seen by humans as well as gods. This is a fantasy perhaps, but it is a fantasy most of us are addicted to.[37]

Cinema has fuelled our addiction to this fantasy. There are good reasons to pursue the 'metaphorical afterlife' of the oracle in relation to Godard. No other filmmaker has had his utterances pored over as much as Godard, whose *aperçus*, aphorisms and pronouncements have become so much part of his work that they have almost come to stand in for it. And in the case of the later work, poorly distributed and frequently consigned to word-of-mouth circulation alone, they seem almost to have replaced it altogether. It's safe to say, though, that Godard's art comprises his work as well as his own commentary on it. But, as Michael Witt points out, '[B]efore either glibly dismissing or appropriating Godard's aphorisms, we should be alert to the fact that, far from an unconnected kaleidoscopic collage of miscellany, these formulae have a context and come with a history.'[38] But underlying the context and the history is the abiding relationship of Godard to his followers and Godard to cinema. Could one describe this relationship as 'oracular', with Godard's followers consulting him as one would consult an oracle who, in allowing cinema to speak *through* him, claims to speak *for* it? Wood again:

> If an oracle is a form of words and the fulfilment of an oracle consists in the match – some kind of match – between those words and an event, in the future or the present or the past, then the ultimate question about an oracle…is not whether it tells the truth but what we will allow to count as the truth. It is a matter of interpretation but also of reference…[39]

But what if the oracle communicates in a form other than words alone? And will we allow Godard's assertion that cinema 'communicates in advance' to count as the truth? Cinema, Godard speculates in *Fatale beauté*, is 'neither an art, nor a technology, but a mystery'. But then, technology has long been ascribed mysterious powers. Clocks, watches and chronometers forecast change and tell the future and the relationship of oracles to technology is long-standing; from *Gulliver's Travels* – 'He called it [the watch] his oracle, and said it pointed out the time for every action of his life' – to the Oracle teletext system developed in the 1970s and the computer software company of the same name.[40] Consider Lemmy's encounters with Alpha 60. These are partly interrogation sessions, partly oracle consultations in which the machine insists that it will find out who Lemmy is and what he's thinking, rather than the other way round and throughout which boom microphones swing in and out of shot with movements that are both threatening and yet curiously seductive (see Appendix 1, Sequences 5 and 7). This effect derives partly from the smoothly mechanical arcs that the microphones describe, like the movements of miniature cranes. But, while we know that, just out of shot, there is a 'perchman' (as the French call the boom operator) scrupulously guiding the microphones into place, we feel that these microphones swoop automatically at the machine's command. When Godard later reprises these shots, in *Scénario du film 'Passion'* (1982) and throughout *Histoire(s) du cinéma*, it's no longer Lemmy who's in the hot seat but the director himself. Here, Godard bids his machines – his video monitors and film reels, his electronic typewriter and projection screen, all the technical paraphernalia of cinema he has gathered around him in his home studio in Switzerland – to respond to him, to reveal their mysteries in sounds and images.

'The oracle' is a persona that the director has assumed with humorous solemnity over the past 20 or so years, the former *enfant terrible* having become the elderly *idiot savant*. Of course, it's part of Godard's schtick, an only semi-humorous *mise en scène* for propositions that are serious and, indeed, mysterious. And, while he has been sonorously mourning 'the death' of cinema throughout this period, his attendant melancholy at cinema's slow-fade demise has done nothing to prevent him from continuing to work. The cinema screen may well be slowly growing darker (there are so many black screens in his late films, it is as though the apparatus itself was lapsing in and out of repose) but the soundworld of his films is richer and denser than ever. Listen carefully and you can just make out a few words, a communication in code that the oracle conveys to us from its mysterious source, the capital city of a distant star: 'There are times when reality becomes too complex for oral transmission. But legend gives it a form by which it pervades the whole world.' It's up to us to work out what they mean.

Notes

The image at the opening of this chapter is a photograph of a light sculpture by the Italian–Scottish artist Belinda Guidi, entitled *Alphaville* (2002), which was exhibited as an installation as part of the show 'International Business Machines' at the Centre for Contemporary Arts in Glasgow, November 2002 to January 2003. Dimensions of the largest ring: 2.30m x 2.30m x 12cm. Materials: steel, aluminum, plastics, electric wiring, economy light bulbs, motor.

1 http://www.alphavilleherald.com. This website documents activities in the virtual world of Alphaville, the biggest city in The Sims Online, a spin-off of the successful Sims computer game. *The Alphaville Herald* was the city's newspaper, the chief reporter on which was Urizenus, the avatar of Peter Ludlow, a philosophy professor at the University of Michigan. But, as the BBC reported, 'as the problems of the Sims Online mounted, *The Alphaville Herald* – which exists as a separate website – became a guidebook to the goings-on in this dystopia. Mr.Ludlow thought the people behind the game should know what was going on inside Alphaville, not least because some things – child prostitution, for example – are morally and legally troubling. But when they found out, Maxis, the game's developers, and Electronic Arts, the distributors, banned all in-game mention of *The Alphaville Herald*, says Mr.Ludlow.' In Ward, Mark, The Dark Side of Digital Utopia' http://news.bbc.co.uk/2/hi/technology/3334923.stm (accessed January 2004).

2 Interview with Peter Whitehead, 25 February 2004.

3 Ibid.

4 Whitehead exaggerates somewhat regarding Godard's treatment for *Alphaville*. The director was famous for generally refusing to write scripts but often produced detailed treatments. Interview with Whitehead.

5 Newspaper reviewers tended to agree that the combination of Scanner's 'invasive' sound surgery and the anamorphic projection was to the film's detriment. In *The Guardian*, Jonathan Romney observed that Scanner 'undermines the film's feat of conceptual *trompe l'oeil*: *Alphaville* seems to show us an alien sci-fi world, whereas in fact Godard is simply shooting a future-obsessed 1965 Paris. Emphasising futurism, rather than the sense of present-as-future, Scanner's electronica makes the film seem archaic, another of those fanciful *Tomorrow's World* projections that date sci-fi so quickly.' Writing in *The Times*, Hettie Judah dismissed the entire venture with a shudder as 'a genuinely unpleasant, even nauseating, experience'.

6 The description is given by Fritz Lang in *Le Mépris*.

7 'Paris-Godard: la ville, la politique, le langage', Swiss Cultural Centre, 4 November 2000–7 January 2001.

8 'Mnemotechnics' is the term used to describe 'an art of memory [which] seeks to memorise through a technique of impressing "places" and "images" on memory': Yates, Frances A., *The Art of Memory* (University of Chicago Press, Chicago, 1966), p. xi.

9 Interview with Chris Marker, 28 November 2003.

10 Bellour, Raymond, 'The book, back and forth', in L. Roth and R. Bellour (eds), *Qu'est-ce qu'une Madeleine? À propos du CD-ROM Immemory de Chris Marker* (Yves Gevaert Éditeur and Centre Georges Pompidou, Geneva and Paris, 1997), p. 145. Translated by B. Holmes.

11 Ibid. pp. 145–146.

12 See Lee, Min, 'Red skies: joining forces with the militant collective S.L.O.N.', *Film Comment*, July–August 2003, pp. 38–41.

13 For those thinking this might be the only new wave sci-fi double bill, what about *Fahrenheit 451* (François Truffaut, 1966) and *La Brûlure de mille soleils* (Pierre Kast, 1965)?

14 Possessing what Michel Chion has described as a 'voice that sees', Alpha 60 predates Kubrick's HAL in *2001: A Space Odyssey*, the deranged super-

computer with the troublingly emollient tones, while also descending from the hypnotic power of Mabuse's disembodied voice in *The Testament of Dr Mabuse/Das Testament des Dr Mabuse* (Fritz Lang, 1932): Chion, Michel, *The Voice in Cinema* (Columbia University Press, New York, 1999), p. 33, translated by C. Gorbman.

15 Romney, Jonathan, 'Stop making sense', *Sight and Sound,* May 2004.

16 Ballard, *A User's Guide to the Millennium,* 1996, p. 192.

17 Williams, James S., 'European culture and artistic resistance in *Histoire(s) du cinéma 3A La monnaie de l'absolu*', in M. Temple and J.S. Williams (eds), *The Cinema Alone: Essays on the Work of Jean-Luc Godard 1985–2000* (Amsterdam University Press, Amsterdam, 2000), pp. 114–115.

18 The film's title translates literally as *Germany Year 90 Nine Zero* but the word 'neuf' can also mean 'new'. The title also refers to Roberto Rossellini's *Germany, Year Zero/Germania, Anno Zero* (1947), set in the ruins of post-war Germany.

19 The phrase is a reference to Constantine's pre-*Alphaville* appearances as Lemmy Caution, 'O, les salauds!' being his frequent exclamation and catchphrase.

20 *Vent d'Est* (*Wind from the East,* 1970) is the title of one of Godard's films from his Dziga Vertov Group phase made in collaboration with Jean-Pierre Gorin. Eddie Constantine's son, named Lemmy, appears in *Éloge de l'amour* playing a lawyer.

21 Benjamin, Walter, 'Theses on the philosophy of history', in H. Arendt (ed.), *Illuminations,* translated by H. Zohn (Shocken Books, New York, 1969), pp. 257–258.

22 Rosenbaum, Jonathan, *Review of Éloge de l'amour*, http://www.chireader.com/movies/archives/2002/1002/021018.html (accessed May 2004).

23 Martin, Adrian, *Review of Éloge de l'amour*, http://www.realtimearts.net/rt50/godard.html (accessed May 2004).

24 Godard, Jean-Luc, 'Le Cinéma est fait pour penser l'impensable', in Bergala, *Jean-Luc Godard par Jean-Luc Godard,* vol. 2, p. 296.

25 Dugas, Lucie, '*Allemagne année 90 neuf zéro:* La mémoire fait l'histoire', *CinémAction* 109, 2003, p. 33.

26 Nicole Brenez proposes a reading of this sequence as part of the film's overall colour scheme being based around the colour white: Brenez, Nicole, 'Le film abymé: Jean-Luc Godard et les philosophies byzantines de l'image', in M. Cerisuelo (ed.), *Jean-Luc Godard, au-delà de l'image* Études cinématographiques no. 194–202 (Lettres Modernes, Paris, 1993), pp. 135–163.

27 The son of the god Apollo and the muse Calliope, Orpheus sang of his beloved Eurydice, who had died of a snake's bite. His song was so sweet that it gained him entrance to the underworld, from which he was granted permission to leave with Eurydice, on the condition that he did not look back at her throughout their journey. His patience failed him and Eurydice was condemned to death. See Graves, Robert, *The Greek Myths* (Penguin, London, 1992), pp. 111–115.

28 Godard, Jean-Luc, 'Entretien', p. 222. The reference to 'death at work' is indeed in *Orphée* but is used to describe mirrors rather than cinema: 'Each time you look into a mirror,' Heurtebise tells the poet, 'you will see death at work there, like a hive of bees in a glass.'

29 Wood, Michael, *The Road to Delphi: The Life and Afterlife of Oracles* (Farrar, Strauss and Giroux, New York, 2003), p. 63.

30 Aumont, Jacques, 'Orphée se retournant', in J. Aumont (ed.), *Amnésies: Fictions d'après Jean-Luc Godard* (P.O.L. Éditeur, Paris, 1999), p. 36.
31 Ibid. p. 39.
32 Ibid. pp. 40–41.
33 Ibid. p. 37.
34 The *Lichtdom*, or cathedral of light, was a highly popular and effective feature of Nazi rallies at Nuremberg between 1934 and 1938. Conceived by Albert Speer, Hitler's architect, to give spatial structure to the night sky, the display involved casting the beams of hundreds of searchlights upwards all focused on a single point. The *Lichtdom* features in *Triumph of the Will* (Leni Riefenstahl, 1935) and was originally developed by Speer 'in order to mask the fact that the middle-aged party members, whose night-time ceremony it originally dramatized, could not be expected to maintain the military discipline displayed by the army and the S.A.'. In James-Chakraborty, Kathleen, 'The drama of illumination: visions of community from Wilhelmine to Nazi Germany', in R.A. Etlin (ed.), *Art, Culture and Media Under The Third Reich* (University of Chicago Press, Chicago and London, 2002), p. 181.
35 Karl Freund was the cinematographer on key films of the German silent cinema of the 1920s, including *Metropolis* (Fritz Lang, 1927) and *The Last Laugh/Der Letzte Mann* (F.W. Murnau, 1924).
36 Witt, Michael, 'Montage, my beautiful care, or histories of the cinematograph', in Temple and Williams (eds), *The Cinema Alone*, p. 45.
37 Wood, *The Road to Delphi*, p. 50.
38 Witt, Michael, '"Qu'était-ce que le cinéma, Jean-Luc Godard?" An analysis of the cinema(s) at work in and around Godard's *Histoire(s) du cinéma*', in E. Ezra, and S. Harris (eds), *France in Focus: Film and National Identity* (Berg, Oxford and New York, 2000,), p. 38.
39 Wood, *The Road to Delphi*, p. 99.
40 Swift, Jonathan, *Gulliver's Travels* (Oxford University Press, Oxford and New York, 1986), part 1, chap. 2, p. 21.

Appendix 1: Sequence breakdown

Sequence 1: Lemmy's arrival (Chapters 1 and 2)

With shots of a flashing light, a white car drives through the peripheral roads and streets of a city at night. At the wheel is Lemmy Caution. He drives to his hotel, where he registers as Ivan Johnson, a reporter from the *Figaro-Pravda* newspaper. Lemmy is shown to his room by a blonde *séductrice*, named Béatrice, who offers herself to him. He refuses her advances and hears a voice echo through his room, warning him to be polite. The voice is that of a policeman who is in Lemmy's bathroom; a fight ensues, with Lemmy shooting at the cop as he flees. Lemmy expels Béatrice from his room and receives word from the reception that 'Miss Natasha von Braun' is on her way up to visit him.

Sequence 2: Natasha von Braun (Chapter 2)

Natasha von Braun arrives at Lemmy's door. He lights her cigarette. She tells him that she is to be his escort while he is in the city and invites him to a gala reception. He tells her he will join her later as he has some business to attend to first. They leave together. As they walk down the corridor together, Lemmy is surprised to learn that Natasha doesn't know the meaning of the word 'love'. Together, they take a taxi through the night-time streets of Alphaville, and, during the journey, Lemmy learns that Natasha is the daughter of the renegade scientist Professor von Braun. Lemmy stops at a building to make a telecommunication, where he is attacked by a knife-wielding cop, whom he kills.

Sequence 3: Henry Dickson at the Red Star hotel (Chapters 1 and 2)

Lemmy arrives at a run-down building, the Red Star hotel, where he waits in the lobby for one of the residents, Henry Dickson, a former spy. Henry arrives and has trouble recognising Lemmy. As they climb the stairs to Henry's room he collapses, wheezing. In Henry's room, Lemmy watches from a hiding place while Henry attempts to make love to a *séductrice* then writhes in agony. Lemmy rushes to his side as Henry, with his dying breath, instructs Lemmy to destroy Alpha 60 and indicates a book hidden beneath his pillow. It is a book of poetry: *Capitale de la douleur*.

Sequence 4: The Institute of General Semantics and the gala reception (Chapters 1, 2 and 3)

Lemmy takes a taxi to the Institute of General Semantics, where he is due to meet Natasha. Lemmy walks into a seminar room, where, in the dark, he listens to a lecture by Alpha 60 in the company of a group of other people, including Natasha. Lemmy leaves the lecture before it's over. Natasha joins him later in the lobby and explains the lecture to him. They travel together to the Gala reception, which takes place at a swimming pool and consists of several dissidents being executed. Lemmy recognises Professor von Braun as one of those attending and asks Natasha to introduce him to her father. When Lemmy tries forcefully to talk to the professor he is beaten unconscious by his bodyguards.

Sequence 5: Alpha 60 and the first interrogation (Chapters 2 and 3)

Lemmy comes round while being dragged down a corridor on his way to being interrogated by Alpha 60. While the computer is processing Lemmy's responses to its questions, the Chief Engineer shows him around the nerve centre of Alphaville, during which it is announced that Alphaville has declared war on Lemmy's country, the Outerlands. In the ensuing confusion, Lemmy escapes.

Sequence 6: Lemmy and Natasha's love scene (Chapter 2)

Back at his hotel, Lemmy finds Natasha waiting for him in his room. Reading from the book Henry gave him, he asks her whether she recognises any of the words (banned by the Alphaville authorities) in the poems. He also questions her about where she was born. Natasha tells him that she wants to return with him to the Outerlands, and Lemmy admits that he is in love with her. As they share rhapsodic moments of love, a police car pulls up outside the hotel.

Sequence 7: The second interrogation, the destruction of Alphaville and the lovers escape (Chapters 2 and 3)

The police arrive in Lemmy's room and, after assessing his guilt, take him for a further interrogation session with Alpha 60. The computer knows his real identity but Lemmy sets the machine a riddle that, when solved, will guarantee its destruction. Shooting his way out of the interrogation room, Lemmy sets off to find Professor von Braun, only to see Natasha being dragged into the building as he leaves. Locating the Professor, Lemmy tries to bargain with him, but ends up shooting him and firing bullets into the computer. After a struggle with an Alphaville thug and a car chase, Lemmy frees Natasha from her captivity, and, as inhabitants of the city stagger around them, the couple make their way to Lemmy's car. With Alpha 60 in meltdown and the city on the verge of destruction, Lemmy and Natasha drive away towards the Outerlands.

Appendix 2: Credits

Alphaville, une étrange aventure de Lemmy Caution
1965, France/Italy
35mm 98 mins
Released in Paris, 5 May 1965

Crew

Director: Jean-Luc Godard
Screenplay: Jean-Luc Godard
Dialogue: Jean-Luc Godard
Production companies: Chaumiane Productions (France); Filmstudio (Italy)
Producer: André Michelin
Director of production: Philippe Dussart
Distributor: Athos Films
Director of photograph: Raoul Coutard
Camera operator: Georges Liron
Camera assistant: Jean Garcenot
Unit manager: Maurice Urbain
Administration: Henry Dutrannoy
Supervising gaffer: Fernand Coquet
Production secretary: Jeanne-Marie Liron
Key grip: Bernard Largemains
Grip: Roger Schleich
Sound engineer: René Levert
Music: Paul Misraki
Assistant directors: Jean-Paul Savignac; Charles L. Bitsch
Second assistant directors: Hélène Kalouguine; Jean-Pierre Léaud
Trainee director: Jacques Barzaghi
Script supervisor: Suzanne Schiffman
Editor: Agnès Guillemot
Assistant editor: Delphine Desfons
Props: Joseph Gerhard; Pierre Clauzel
Costumes: Laurence Clairval; Yvonne Garetier
Make-up: Jackie Reynal
Hairstyles: Lionel
On-set photographer: Georges Pierre
Stills: Marilu Parolini

Cast

Eddie Constantine: Lemmy Caution; Anna Karina: Natasha von Braun; Akim Tamiroff: Henry Dickson; Howard Vernon: Professor Leonard Nosferatu/von Braun; Michel Delahaye: von Braun's assistant; Laszlo Szabo: Chief Engineer; Jean-André Fieschi: Professor Heckell; Jean-Louis Comolli: Professor Jeckell; also featuring: Christa Lang; Jean-Pierre Léaud

Appendix 3: Filmography

2001: A Space Odyssey (Stanley Kubrick, 1968)
À Bout de souffle/Breathless (Jean-Luc Godard, 1960)
Alien (Ridley Scott, 1979)
Allemagne 90 année neuf zéro/Germany Year 90 Nine Zero (Jean-Luc Godard, 1991)
Alphaville, une étrange aventure de Lemmy Caution/Alphaville, a strange adventure of Lemmy Caution (Jean-Luc Godard, 1965)
Anticipation, ou l'amour en l'an 2000 (Jean-Luc Godard, 1967), in *Le plus vieux métier du monde/The World's Oldest Profession* (various, 1967)
Blade Runner (Ridley Scott, 1982)
Bonnie and Clyde (Arthur Penn, 1967)
Das Cabinet des Dr Caligari/The Cabinet of Dr Caligari (Robert Weine, 1919)
Caméra Oeil/Camera Eye (Jean-Luc Godard, 1967), in *Loin de Vietnam/Far from Vietnam* (Godard, Marker, Ivens, Varda, Resnais, Lelouch, Klein, 1967)
Code 46 (Michael Winterbottom, 2003)
Confidential Report/Mr Arkadin (Orson Welles, 1955)
Cypher (Vincenzo Natali, 2002)
Dark City (Alex Proyas, 1998)
Das Testament des Dr Mabuse/The Testament of Dr Mabuse (Fritz Lang, 1932)
DemonLover (Olivier Assayas, 2002)
Der Müde Tod/Destiny (Fritz Lang, 1921)
Détective (Jean-Luc Godard, 1984)
Deux ou trois choses que je sais d'elle/Two or Three Things I Know About Her (Jean-Luc Godard, 1967)
Dr Strangelove, or, How I Learned to Stop Worrying and Love the Bomb (Stanley Kubrick, 1964)
Éloge de l'amour/In Praise of Love (Jean-Luc Godard, 2001)
Fahrenheit 451 (François Truffaut, 1966)
Fatale beauté, Episode 2B Histoire(s) du cinéma (Jean-Luc Godard, 1989–1998)
Faust (F.W. Murnau, 1926)
Gattaca (Andrew Niccol, 1997)
Germania, Anno Zero/Germany, Year Zero (Roberto Rossellini, 1947)
Gertrud (Carl Theodor Dreyer, 1964)
Goldfinger (Guy Hamilton, 1964)
Hélas pour moi/Oh, Woe is Me (Jean-Luc Godard, 1993)
Hiroshima mon amour (Alain Resnais, 1959)
Histoire(s) du cinéma (Jean-Luc Godard, 1989–1998)
Immemory (Chris Marker, 1997, CD-ROM)
Jaws (Steven Spielberg, 1977)
King Lear (Jean-Luc Godard, 1987)

Kiss Me Deadly (Robert Aldrich, 1955)
L'Atalante (Jean Vigo, 1934)
La Bête humaine (Jean Renoir, 1938)
La Brûlure de mille soleils (Pierre Kast, 1965)
La Chinoise (Jean-Luc Godard, 1967)
Le Gendarme de Saint-Tropez/The Gendarme of Saint Tropez (Jean Girault, 1964)
La Jetée (Chris Marker, 1962)
Le Mépris/Contempt (Jean-Luc Godard, 1963)
La Môme vert-de-gris/Poison Ivy (Bernard Borderie, 1952)
Le nouveau monde/The New World (Jean-Luc Godard, 1963) in *RoGoPaG* (Rossellini, Godard, Pasolini, Gregoretti, 1962)
La Paresse/Sloth (Jean-Luc Godard, 1962), in *Les sept péchés capitaux/The Seven Deadly Sins* (various, 1961)
La Passion de Jeanne d'Arc/The Passion of Joan of Arc (Carl Theodor Dreyer, 1928)
Le petit soldat/The Little Soldier (Jean-Luc Godard, 1960)
Le Silence de la mer (Jean-Pierre Melville, 1949)
Les Carabiniers/The Riflemen (Jean-Luc Godard, 1963)
Les Vacances de M. Hulot/Monsieur Hulot's Holidays (Jacques Tati, 1953)
Made in USA (Jean-Luc Godard, 1966)
Masculin-Féminin (Jean-Luc Godard, 1966)
Mauvais sang/The Night is Young (Leos Carax, 1986)
Metropolis (Fritz Lang, 1927)
Minority Report (Steven Spielberg, 2002)
Moi, un noir (Jean Rouch, 1958)
Nosferatu: eine Symphonie des Grauens (F.W. Murnau, 1922)
On the Beach (Stanley Kramer, 1959)
Orphée (Jean Cocteau, 1949)
Passion (Jean-Luc Godard, 1982)
Pépé le Moko (Julien Duvivier, 1937)
Pickpocket (Robert Bresson, 1959)
Pierrot le fou (Jean-Luc Godard, 1965)
Playtime (Jacques Tati, 1967)
Point Blank (John Borman, 1967)
Prénom Carmen/First Name: Carmen (Jean-Luc Godard, 1983)
Scarface (Howard Hawks, 1932)
Scénario du film 'Passion' (Jean-Luc Godard, 1982)
Seul le cinéma, Episode 2A Histoire(s) du cinéma (Jean-Luc Godard, 1989–1998)
Sib/The Apple (Samira Makmalbaf, 1998)
The Awful Dr Orlof /Gritos en la noche (Jesus Franco, 1962)
The General Died at Dawn (Lewis Milestone, 1936)
The Golem/Der Golem, wie er in die Welt kam (Paul Wegener, 1920)
The Last Laugh/Der Letzte Mann (F.W. Murnau, 1924)
The Long Goodbye (Robert Altman, 1973)
The Matrix (Andy Wachowski and Larry Wachowski, 1999)
The Thousand Eyes of Dr Mabuse/Die Tausend Augen des Dr Mabuse (Fritz Lang, 1960)
The Trial (Orson Welles, 1963)
The World, the Flesh and the Devil (Ranald Mac Dougall, 1959)
THX 1138 (George Lucas, 1971)

To Have and Have Not (Howard Hawks, 1944)
Tonite Let's All Make Love in London (Peter Whitehead, 1967)
Touch of Evil (Orson Welles, 1958)
Triumph des Willens/Triumph of the Will (Leni Riefenstahl, 1935)
Une Femme est une femme/A Woman is a Woman (Jean-Luc Godard, 1961)
Une Femme mariée/A Married Woman (Jean-Luc Godard, 1964)
Une Vague nouvelle, Episode 3B Histoire(s) du cinéma (Jean-Luc Godard, 1989–1998)
Vampyr: l'étrange aventure de David Gray (Carl Theodor Dreyer, 1932)
Vent d'Est/Wind from the East (Jean-Luc Godard, Jean-Pierre Gorin, 1970)
Weekend (Jean-Luc Godard, 1967)
Wholly Communion (Peter Whitehead, 1965)

Appendix 4: Select bibliography

Abrams, M.H., *The Mirror and the Lamp: Romantic Theory and the Critical Tradition* (Oxford University Press, New York, 1953).
Ajame, Pierre, 'Alphaville: entretien avec Eddie Constantine', *Les Nouvelles Littéraires,* 1 April 1965.
Amengual, Barthélemy, *Bande à part de Jean-Luc Godard* (Éditions Yellow Now, Belgium, 1993).
Amis, Kingsley, *New Maps of Hell* (Victor Gollancz, London, 1960).
Andreu, Anna and Garrigou-Lagrange, Madeleine, 'Alphaville', *Témoignage chrétien,* 21 May 1965.
Andreu, Anne, *Paris-presse,* 12 May 1965.
Ardagh, John, *The New French Revolution: A Social and Economic Survey of France 1945–1967* (Secker and Warburg, London, 1968).
Augé, Marc, *Non-Places: Introduction to an Anthropology of Supermodernity* (Verso, London and New York, 1995).
Aumont, Jacques, *Amnésies: Fictions d'après Jean-Luc Godard* (P.O.L. Éditeur, Paris, 1999).
Aumont, Jacques, *Du Visage au cinéma* (Éditions de l'Étoile/Cahiers du cinéma, Paris, 1992).
Baby, Yvonne, 'Dresser des embuscades dans le planification', *Le Monde,* 6 May 1965.
Ballard, J.G., *A User's Guide to the Millennium* (HarperCollins, London, 1996).
Bandy, Mary Lea and Bellour, Raymond (eds), *Jean-Luc Godard: Son + Image, 1974–1991* (Museum of Modern Art, New York, 1992).
Bellour, Raymond, 'The book, back and forth', in L. Roth and R. Bellour (eds), *Qu'est-ce qu'une Madeleine? À propos du CD-ROM Immemory de Chris Marker* (Yves Gevaert Éditeur and Centre Georges Pompidou, Geneva and Paris, 1997).
Benayoun, Robert, 'Alphaville – la nébuleuse de l'épate-bourgeois', *Positif* 71, 1965.
Benjamin, Walter, 'Theses on the philosophy of history', in H. Arendt (ed.), *Illuminations,* translated by H. Zohn (Shocken Books, New York, 1969).
Bergala, Alain (ed.), *Jean-Luc Godard par Jean-Luc Godard,* vol. 1, *1950–1984* (Cahiers du cinéma, Paris, 1998).
Bergala, Alain (ed.), *Jean-Luc Godard par Jean-Luc Godard,* vol. 2, *1984–1998* (Cahiers du cinéma, Paris, 1998).
Bertolucci, Bernardo, 'Versus Godard', *Cahiers du cinéma* 186, 1967.
Black, Edwin, *IBM and the Holocaust: The Strategic Alliance between Nazi Germany and America's Most Powerful Corporation* (Time Warner Books, London, 2002).
Bodanis, David, *$E=mc^2$: A Biography of the World's Most Famous Equation* (Macmillan, London, 2000).
Borde, Raymond and Chaumeton, Etienne, *Panorama du film noir américain* (Editions de minuit, Paris, 1955).

Bory, Jean-Louis, 'Alphaville: Terrible!', in *Des Yeux pour voir: Cinéma 1 1961–1966* (Union Générale d'Éditions, Paris, 1971).
Bower, Tom, *The Paperclip Conspiracy: The Battle for the Spoils and Secrets of Nazi Germany* (Michael Joseph, London, 1987).
Boyle, Nicholas, *Goethe: The Poet and the Age* vol. 1: *The Poetry of Desire 1749–1790* (Clarendon Press, Oxford, 1991).
Burgess, Anthony, *Nineteen-Eighty Five* (Arrow Books, London, 1980).
Cahiers du cinéma 505, 1996, 'Howard Vernon: d'Orlaf à Hermocrate'.
Cameron, Ian (ed.), *The Films of Jean-Luc Godard* (Studio Vista, London, 1967).
Carey, John, *The Faber Book of Utopias* (Faber and Faber, London, 1999).
Cerisuelo, Marc, *Jean-Luc Godard* (Éditions des Quatre-Vents, Paris, 1989).
Cerisuelo, Marc (ed.), *Jean-Luc Godard, au-delà de l'image,* Étude cinématographique no. 194–202 (Lettres Modernes, Paris, 1993).
Cerisuelo, Marc, 'Godard et la théorie: tu n'as rien vu à Pesaro', *CinémAction* 109, 2003.
Chapier, Henri, 'Le Pari Romantique de Jean-Luc Godard', *Combat,* 8 May 1965.
Chapier, Henri, 'Oui a Robbe-Grillet et non à Antonioni et Godard', *Combat* 5, July 1965.
Chion, Michel, *The Voice in Cinema,* translated by C. Gorbman (Columbia University Press, New York, 1999).
Comolli, Jean-Louis, 'A rebours?', *Cahiers du cinéma* 168, July 1965.
Copjec, Joan (ed.), *Shades of Noir* (London, Verso, 1993).
Cournot, Michel, 'Les Robots sonts déjà là', *Le Nouvel Observateur* 25, 1965.
D'Allones, Fabrice Revault, *La Lumière au cinéma* (Cahiers du cinéma, Paris, 1991).
Darke, Chris, 'It all Happened in Paris', *Sight and Sound,* June 1994.
Daussois, Guy, 'Alphaville: découvrir notre univers de demain', *Démocratie* 60 (6), 1965.
Dawkins, Richard, *Unweaving the Rainbow: Science, Delusion and the Appetite for Wonder* (Allen Lane, London, 1998).
Dort, Bernard, 'Godard ou le Romantique abusif', *Les Temps Modernes,* December 1965.
Douchet, Jean, 'Le théorème de Godard', *Cahiers du cinéma* 'spécial' 'Godard: 30 ans depuis', November 1990.
Douin, Jean-Luc, *Jean-Luc Godard* (Rivages, Paris, 1989).
Dugas, Lucie, '*Allemagne année 90 neuf zéro:* la mémoire fait l'histoire', *CinémAction* 109, 2003.
Eisner, Lotte H., *L'Ecran démoniaque: Influence de Max Reinhardt et de l'expressionisme* (Éditions André Bonne, Paris, 1952).
Elkaïm, Arlette, 'Alphaville ou Bétafilm?', *Les Temps Modernes* 229, 1965.
Elsaesser, Thomas, '*Alphaville*' *Brighton Film Review,* 1 April 1969.
Elsaesser, Thomas (ed.), *Weimar Cinema and After: Germany's Historical Imaginary* (Routledge, London and New York, 2000).
Etlin, Richard A. (ed.), *Art, Culture and Media Under The Third Reich* (University of Chicago Press, Chicago and London, 2002).
Evenson, Norma, *Paris: A Century of Change, 1878–1978* (Yale University Press, New Haven, CT and London, 1979).
Ezra, Elizabeth and Harris, Sue (eds), *France in Focus: Film and National Identity* (Berg, Oxford and New York, 2000).
Farber, Manny, *Negative Space: Manny Farber on the Movies* (Da Capo Press, New York, 1998).

Farocki, Harun and Silverman, Kaja, *Speaking About Godard* (New York University Press, New York, 1998).
France Nouvelle, 12 May 1965.
Frayn, Michael, *Copenhagen* (Methuen, London, 2003).
Godard, Jean-Luc, 'L'Afrique vous parle de la fin et des moyens', *Cahiers du cinéma* 94, 1959.
Godard, Jean-Luc, 'Entretien: les *Cahiers* rencontreu Godard après ses quatre premiers films', *Cahiers du cinéma* 138, 1962.
Godard, Jean-Luc, 'Trois mille heures de cinéma', *Cahiers du cinéma* 184, 1966.
Godard, Jean-Luc, 'Lutter sur deux fronts', *Cahiers du cinéma* 194, 1967.
Godard, Jean-Luc, 'One or two things: Jean-Luc Godard', *Sight and Sound*, Winter 1966/1967.
Godard, Jean-Luc, *Introduction à une véritable histoire du cinéma* (Éditions Albatros, Paris, 1980).
Godard, Jean-Luc, 'Le Cinéma est fait pour penser l'impensable', in A. Bergala (ed.), *Jean-Luc Godard par Jean-Luc Godard*, vol. 2, 1984–1998 (Cahiers du cinéma, Paris, 1998).
Godard, Jean-Luc, *Alphaville: A Film by Jean-Luc Godard* (Faber and Faber, London, 2000).
Graves, Robert, *The Greek Myths* (Penguin, London, 1992).
Gross, Larry, 'Film après noir', *Film Quarterly*, July–August 1976.
Hammond, Paul, *The Shadow and its Shadow: Surrealist Writings on Cinema* (British Film Institute, London, 1978).
Hansard, 12 March 1868, 1517/1.
Hillegas, Mark R., *The Future as Nightmare: H.G. Wells and the Anti-utopians* (Oxford University Press, New York, 1967).
Hollywood Reporter, 23 September 1977.
Huxley, Aldous, *Brave New World* (Penguin, London, 1955).
Jackson, Kevin, 'The divine Miss K gets real', *The Independent*, 29 June 2001.
Jacob, Gilles, 'Alphaville: for or against', *Sight and Sound*, Winter 1965/1966.
Jacob, Gilles, 'Alphaville: un cauchemar non climatisé', *Cinéma* 65 (8), 1965.
Jay, Martin, *Downcast Eyes: The Denigration of Vision in Twentieth-Century French Thought* (University of California Press, Berkeley, 1993).
Jencks, Charles, *Modern Movements in Architecture* (Penguin, London and New York, 1973).
Kracauer, Seigfried, *From Caligari to Hitler: A Psychological History of the German Film* (L'Age d'homme, Lausanne, 1947).
Lachize, Samuel, 'Lemmy aux Enfers', *L'Humanité*, 9 May 1965.
MacCabe, Colin, *Godard: Images, Sounds, Politics* (British Film Institute and Macmillan, London, 1980).
MacCabe, Colin, *Godard: A Portrait of the Artist at 70* (Bloomsbury, London, 2003).
Marcuse, Herbert, *One-Dimensional Man: Studies in the Ideology of Advanced Industrial Society* (Routledge and Kegan Paul, London, 1984).
Marie, Michel, *À Bout de souffle étude critique* (Éditions Nathan, Paris, 1999).
Marker, Chris, 'Marker direct', *Film Comment*, May–June 2003.
Martin, Adrian, 'Recital: three lyrical interludes in Godard', in J. Williams, M. Witt, and M. Temple (eds), *Forever Godard* (Black Dog Publishing, London, 2004).

Michelson, Annette, 'Film and the radical aspiration', in P.A. Sitney (ed.), *Film Culture: An Anthology* (Secker and Warburg, London, 1971).
Mumford, Lewis, *The Myth of the Machine: The Pentagon of Power* (Secker and Warburg, London, 1964).
Naremore, James, *More than Night: Film Noir in its Contexts* (University of California Press, Berkeley and London, 1998).
Negley, Glen and Patrick, J. Max, *The Quest for Utopia: An Anthology of Imaginary Societies* (McGrath Publishing Company, College Park, MD, 1971).
Perez, Gilberto, *The Material Ghost: Films and their Medium* (Johns Hopkins University Press, Baltimore and London, 1998).
Pirenne, M.H., *Optics, Painting and Photography* (Cambridge University Press, London and New York, 1970).
Prédal, René, 'Alphaville', *Jeune Cinéma* 8, 1965.
Rochefort, Christiane, *Les petits enfants du siècle* (Grasset, Paris, 1961).
Romney, Jonathan, 'Stop making sense', *Sight and Sound,* May 2004.
Ropars-Wuilleumier, Marie-Claire, 'Loss of language', *Wide Angle* 1 (3), 1976.
Rosenbaum, Jonathan, *Placing Movies: The Practice of Film Criticism* (University of California Press, Berkeley and London, 1995).
Ross, Kristin, *Fast Cars, Clean Bodies: Decolonization and the Reordering of French Culture* (MIT Press, Cambridge, MA and London, 1995).
Roud, Richard, *Godard* (Thames and Hudson, London, 1970).
Roud, Richard, 'Anguish: Alphaville', in J.L. Godard, *Alphaville: A Film by Jean-Luc Godard,* translation of screenplay by P. Whitehead (Faber and Faber, London, 2000).
Roussel, Bertrand, 'Courbes et subversion esthétique: une approche plastique d'Alphaville', *CinémAction* 52, 1989.
Sadoul, Georges, 'À l'indicatif présent', *Les Lettres Françaises* 13, 1965.
Samson, Pierre, 'À propos d'Alphaville: les mécanismes d'une imposture', *Les Temps Modernes* 230, 1965.
Schlemmer, Isabelle, 'Alphaville', *Jeune Cinéma* 8, June/July 1965.
Silverman, Kaja and Farocki, Harun, *Speaking about Godard* (New York University Press, New York, 1998).
Sontag, Susan, 'The imagination of disaster', in S. Sontag, *Against Interpretation and Other Essays* (Farrar, Strauss and Giroux, New York, 1968).
Sorlin, Pierre, *European Cinemas and European Societies 1939–1990* (Routledge, London, 1991).
Swift, Jonathan, *Gulliver's Travels* (Oxford University Press, Oxford and New York, 1986).
Temple, Michael, Williams, James S. and Witt, Michael (eds), *Forever Godard* (Black Dog Publishing, London, 2004).
Temple, Michael and Williams, James S. (eds), *The Cinema Alone: Essays on the Work of Jean-Luc Godard 1985–2000* (Amsterdam University Press, Amsterdam, 2000).
Tolstoy, Ivan, *The Knowledge and the Power: Reflections on the History of Science* (Canongate, Edinburgh, 1990).
Vincendeau, Ginette, *Stars and Stardom in French Cinema* (Continuum, London and New York, 2000).
Wake, Sandra and Hayden, Nicola, *Bonnie and Clyde* (Lorrimer, London, 1972).
Walsh, Chad, *From Utopia to Nightmare* (Geoffrey Bles, London, 1962).

Wenders, Wim, *Emotion Pictures: Reflections on the Cinema* (Faber and Faber, London, 1986).
Wollen, Peter, *Paris Hollywood: Writings on Film* (Verso, London and New York, 2002).
Wood, Michael, *The Road to Delphi: The Life and Afterlife of Oracles* (Farrar, Strauss and Giroux, New York, 2003).
Wood, Robin, '*Alphaville*', in I. Cameron (ed.), *The Films of Jean-Luc Godard* (Studio Vista, London, 1967).
Yates, Frances A., *The Art of Memory* (University of Chicago Press, Chicago, 1966).
Zamyatin, Yevgeny, *We*, translated by B. G. Guerney (Penguin, London, 1972).